ANXIETY SURVIVAL GUIDE FOR TEENS

How to Build Skills to Navigate Fear, Worry, and Panic

JULIE HAYES

ISBN: 978-1-962496-13-1

For questions, please reach out to Support@OakHarborPress.com

Please consider leaving a review!

Just visit: OakHarborPress.com/Reviews

FREE BONUS

SCAN TO GET OUR NEXT
BOOK FOR FREE!

Table of Contents

INTRODUCTION

Being a teenager is like embarking on a wild adventure filled with twists, turns, and unexpected challenges that can make your heart race and your mind spin. It's normal to feel a bit uneasy as you navigate the maze of exams, social pressures, and uncertainty that come with growing up. That's where this guide comes in— consider it your trusty sidekick, a friendly voice in your ear offering tips and tricks to help you conquer the anxiety lurking in the shadows.

Inside these pages, you'll discover practical strategies to combat the stressors that might be cramping your style. From coping mechanisms for those nail-biting exam periods to navigating the tricky terrain of social interactions, this guide will help you through it. We'll dive into the art of mindfulness, breathing exercises, and other tools to help you stay grounded when life throws curveballs your way.

Despite its title, this guide isn't just about helping you survive; it's about helping you thrive. We'll explore ways to embrace your uniqueness, build resilience, and turn moments of anxiety into opportunities for growth. You're not alone on this adventure— countless teens are grappling with similar challenges, and here you'll find stories, insights, and wisdom to light your path.

So, if you've ever felt like the weight of the world is on your shoulders or that anxiety is trying to steal your spotlight, fear not. This guide is your secret weapon, your roadmap to reclaiming control and embracing the person you are becoming.

CHAPTER ONE: UNDERSTANDING ANXIETY

WHAT IS ANXIETY?

Let's talk about anxiety — that uncomfortable feeling of unease, worry, or fear that you have probably felt before. Picture this: you've got a big test coming up, or you're about to give a presentation in class. That jittery feeling? That's anxiety, and it's not a bad thing. It's like your brain giving you an extra boost, making you sharp and focused. In a way, it's your body's way of saying, "You've got this!"

Anxiety is totally normal. In fact, it's like our built-in alarm system that kicks in when we face challenges or potential threats. So, when you're feeling a bit anxious, remember — it's not a sign of weakness. It's just you being human. Anxiety is healthy in small doses, but when it starts hanging around too much, it can make life a lot harder than it needs to be.

Sometimes anxiety arises when you're faced with something that makes you nervous; sometimes it might seem to pop up for no reason at all. There are different kinds of anxicty. Many of them — like being anxious before a presentation — are perfectly normal and to be expected. But for some people, anxiety can develop into a serious problem, such as Generalized Anxiety Disorder (GAD).

GAD is a medical condition where the brain won't stop worrying, even when there is really nothing to worry about. Everything — school, friends, the future — causes constant worry and anxiety in

GAD. This condition can also cause symptoms like restlessness, irritability, and muscle tension. If you are ever concerned that your anxiety has gotten out of control, perhaps becoming something like GAD, discuss it with your doctor or a trusted adult, and they can help you find the appropriate treatment.

Even milder forms of anxiety can make life uncomfortable at times. Many people occasionally experience social anxiety, the fear of being judged or embarrassed in social situations. Who hasn't felt a bit awkward at times? Social anxiety can sometimes get so strong that it makes it hard to function, but often it shows up as some nerves before a social event that go away once the event is over.

And, of course, there's "performance" anxiety. This type of anxiety is connected to any time you feel the need to do well, maybe on tests, keeping up with deadlines, or giving a class presentation.

Regardless of which type or types of anxiety you experience, understanding what's behind these feelings is the first step toward conquering them. It can be helpful to talk about it, whether with friends, family, or even a professional. Communication is key and knowing that others have been through the same thing and come out the other side can be very reassuring.

Remember, there's no one-size-fits-all when it comes to anxiety. We're all unique, and our anxiety is influenced by lots of different things: genes, our environments, and how we see the world. Getting help, for example, by talking to a counselor or therapist, can give you some useful tools to deal with anxiety and keep it from taking over.

Knowing that anxiety is a regular part of growing up can be empowering. It means you're not alone, and it's okay to feel this way. Embrace this knowledge, understand your anxiety, and use it as a tool for your own growth. If it ever feels like too much, there are ways to manage it and take control—and that's exactly what this book is going to teach you.

WHY DO TEENS EXPERIENCE ANXIETY?

Being a teenager is not easy. This is a time of exploration, self-discovery, and changes, both internal and external. Experiencing anxiety during these years is not only common but expected. Let's dive into the reasons behind why teens experience anxiety, unpacking this complex journey.

One significant factor in teenage anxiety is the whirlwind of hormonal changes that accompany adolescence. These changes can influence your mood and contribute to feelings of anxiety. It can be hard to manage anxiety caused by hormonal changes. Like other physical changes you notice in your body throughout adolescence and your teenage years, you might feel sometimes like you no longer recognize yourself—the way you look or the way you feel. Again, knowing that this experience is shared by most people and that it is uncomfortable but temporary can help you to get through it.

Academic stress is another likely cause of anxiety for many teens. The transition to high school, SAT prep, finals, and increasingly challenging schoolwork can turn the pursuit of knowledge into a high-pressure situation. A fear of failure, a desire to meet expectations, and pressure about grades can fuel anxiety in the academic realm.

Social dynamics also play a big role in teenage anxiety. Navigating friendships, crushes, and cliques can sometimes feel like walking through a minefield. The fear of judgment, rejection, or not measuring up to societal standards can be overwhelming. Social media doesn't make things any easier, either. Constant comparison of yourself to curated online lives can intensify feelings of inadequacy.

Then there's the family dynamic. While family is a vital support system, it can also be a source of stress for some people. Balancing your growing independence with familial expectations, dealing with conflict, increased accountability, or experiencing changes in family structures can stir up anxiety. A desire for autonomy colliding with a need for support can create conflict between teens and their families that is challenging to handle.

Finally, let's not forget about the future. Your teenage years, while exciting in many ways, can be filled with difficult decisions and a sense of pressure about the future. The looming unknowns surrounding adulthood, career choices, and financial responsibilities might cast a shadow over the present. Questions like "What do I want to do with my life?" or "Can I succeed in my chosen path?" can take up a lot of mental space and energy.

To put it simply, teens experience anxiety because they are navigating a complex maze of internal and external factors, each with its unique set of challenges. It's like trying to juggle multiple balls in the air while riding a unicycle—exhilarating, but also nerve-wracking.

So, how do you deal with all this pressure? For starters, acknowledge that it's okay to feel this way. You're not alone, and your feelings are valid. Talking to someone you trust, whether it's a friend, family member, or counselor, can provide much-needed support. Developing coping mechanisms, like mindfulness or creative outlets, can also be a powerful tool in your anxiety-fighting arsenal.

HOW CAN THIS BOOK HELP?

Being a teenager can feel like surfing rough waves in a storm, and anxiety often makes those waves seem more like tsunamis. That's where this book comes in—this is a guide crafted just for you, filled with insights and practical tips to not only learn what anxiety is all about, but to conquer it too. This book is your go-to tool, created with the help of experts, to navigate the teen years and come out on top. Here are some topics we'll cover:

Getting to Know Anxiety

We'll kick it off by breaking down what anxiety is all about. We give you the lowdown on anxiety in a way that makes sense, helping you understand what you're feeling and why. This guide is your key to understanding and managing this tricky emotion.

Tips and Tricks

Feeling overwhelmed? No worries! This book provides you with real-life tips and tricks to ride out those anxious moments. When you finish reading, you'll have a fully stocked toolkit to wrestle control back from anxiety and show it who's boss.

Boosting Your Mental Muscle

Ever wish you had a superhero mindset? Well, this book is here to help you build resilience and power up a positive attitude. It's like exercise for your brain, turning it into a powerhouse that can handle any emotional curveball life throws your way.

Taking on Anxiety Challenges

Got specific anxiety hang-ups, like stressing in social situations, freaking out during tests, or chasing perfection? We've got your back! This book is packed with game plans to tackle each challenge so you can become the anxiety-busting champ you were born to be.

Managing Panic Attacks

Panic attacks can be really scary. This book lays out strategies to handle those intense moments and eventually kick panic attacks to the curb. You'll basically have a coach in your corner, guiding you through the toughest spots.

Asking for Backup and Building Your Squad

You're not in this alone! We'll show you how to reach out when you need help. It's all about building your own dream team—friends, family, and mentors—who have your back and can help you ride out any storm.

School Hacks and Dealing with Change

School can feel like a jungle, and this book offers a survival guide. From acing exams to facing those nerve-wracking changes, we provide you with the inside scoop on navigating the teen jungle with style.

Facing Fears and Breaking the Avoidance Cycle

Ever feel like avoiding stuff that makes your anxiety spike? This book helps you face those fears head-on, step by step. We'll guide you through confronting your fears one step at a time, helping you reclaim control and conquer anxiety's avoidance grip.

Now, get ready to discover how to defeat anxiety and take charge of your life so that you can become the confident young adult you're meant to be!

SEEKING OUT
HELP

If we stay with the idea that teenage life is like a rollercoaster, then anxiety is that unexpected drop that makes your stomach flip. Sure, self-help books offer some serious knowledge bombs, but here's the real talk—they can only take you so far. When the tips and tricks aren't cutting it, it's totally okay to raise your hand and ask for backup. Seeking help is like leveling up in the game of life, and trust us, it's a power move you won't regret.

Let's break it down. We get it; school stress, social drama, and the whole future thing can be daunting and scary. Those guidebooks? They're like your chill older sibling giving you advice. But sometimes, you need more than words on a page. That's when you tag in the real MVPs—your squad.

Your friends are more than just buddies for gaming marathons or shop-til-you-drop sessions; they're your ride-or-die crew. Odds are, they've faced their own anxiety demons. Sharing your struggles with them is like unlocking a secret level where you can swap stories and have each other's backs. Sharing your story turns anxiety into something you conquer together.

Now, let's talk about the parental units. Yeah, talking to your folks about your feelings can seem awkward, but—spoiler alert—they were teens once too. They've got wisdom to drop and a genuine interest in your well-being. Plus, they can hook you up with pros who specialize in decoding the mysteries of teenage anxiety—therapists and counselors.

Turning to professionals is like bringing in heavy artillery against anxiety. Therapists and counselors tackle anxiety with empathy and kindness. They can handle literally anything you throw at them. They're equipped with tools and tricks to help you conquer anxiety on a whole new level. These pros aren't here to judge; they're here to understand, guide, and collaborate with you to develop a personalized strategy. Think of them as your mental health coaches, ready to assist in leveling up your resilience. Don't underestimate the power of professional help—it's the ultimate game-changer in your anxiety-fighting arsenal.

Not quite ready for the pros yet? No problem. Schools are a treasure trove of resources. School counselors are basically your real-life sidekicks, ready to help you navigate the ups and downs. They're trained to guide you through the maze of teenage emotions, so don't hesitate to ask them for help.

Asking for help isn't a sign that you're not handling life like a boss. It's a flex, a bold move saying, "I got this, but a little backup wouldn't hurt." Teen life is a wild ride, and learning to tackle anxiety head-on is all part of the game. So, don't be shy—your well-being is the ultimate power-up, and seeking help is your super move. You got this!

Activity: Write down one thing that makes you feel anxious and one thing that makes you feel calm.

CHAPTER TWO:
THE MANY FACES
OF ANXIETY

TYPES OF ANXIETY

If you haven't received a diagnosis before picking up this book, it is highly encouraged to talk to your general practitioner about getting tested to see what kind of help is best for you. By now you know that anxiety is a common experience for many teenagers, but you might not know that it comes in various forms. Some anxiety is to be expected; it's a natural part of the human experience. However, other forms of anxiety go beyond that and become really difficult to manage without professional help.

Although the tactics in this book can help manage symptoms, they are not a replacement for proper treatment. Attempting to "white knuckle it" or "just tough it out" will lead to unnecessary discomfort and stress that can easily be relieved with the proper support and medical attention. Understanding the types of anxiety can help you identify what you might be feeling to better help you discuss it with your doctor and obtain the best help possible. Although a little anxiety is typical of the human experience, if you experience any of the below conditions, you'll need additional help from a licensed professional.

Generalized Anxiety Disorder (GAD): This is like having a constant worry cloud hanging over your head. Imagine having a backpack filled with worries, and it never feels like you can take it off, even when things are going well. Teens with GAD often find themselves stressing more than usual about various aspects of life, from school and relationships to future uncertainties. If you think you might have GAD, you can benefit from speaking with a doctor about how to manage this anxiety.

Social Anxiety: Do you ever feel nervous or self-conscious in social situations? That's social anxiety. It bubbles up during things like parties, making you feel like everyone is watching and judging your every move. It can make socializing feel like a big, scary challenge, even if you want to connect with others.

Panic Disorder: Imagine your anxiety hitting you like a ton of bricks out of nowhere. Panic attacks can make your heart race, make it hard to breathe, and create an overwhelming sense of fear. They're often incapacitating. If you experience panic attacks on a rare occasion, you might not need treatment. However, if you've experienced them multiple times, you should seek medical attention and treatment.

Obsessive-Compulsive Disorder (OCD): OCD is like having a broken record playing in your mind. You might have repetitive thoughts or fears (obsessions) that you can't shake, and you might feel compelled to do certain behaviors (compulsions) to ease the anxiety. It's like trying to solve a puzzle that never quite fits together. There are medications and other forms of treatment that can help with OCD; talk with your doctor if you have questions about this condition.

Post-Traumatic Stress Disorder (PTSD): Have you ever experienced something really scary or traumatic? PTSD is when the echoes of that experience seem to haunt you. It can bring back intense feelings, nightmares, or flashbacks, making it challenging to move forward. Children who grew up in abusive homes or with parents in active addiction often suffer from what's known as C-PTSD. The earlier people with these conditions get help, the easier the symptoms are to manage in the long run.

Separation Anxiety: Remember that feeling when you were little, and you didn't want to be away from your parents? Separation anxiety in teenagers is like an exaggerated version of that. It's the worry and fear about being away from loved ones, even when that separation is necessary for your personal growth and independence.

Specific Phobias: Everyone has some things that make them squeamish or nervous, like spiders or heights. Phobias are when these fears of a specific trigger become so intense that they prevent you from living your life to its fullest. Phobias can be about almost anything—flying, swimming, animals, and more.

Health Anxiety (Hypochondria): Ever find yourself worrying excessively about your health, even when there's no clear reason to be concerned? Teens with health anxiety may become preoccupied with the fear of having a serious illness, constantly checking their symptoms or seeking reassurance from others.

Understanding the different types of anxiety helps you recognize and talk about what you're experiencing. Just as there are different types of anxiety, there are different ways to manage and cope with it. The first step is to get a diagnosis, though. You can still read ahead, but the earlier you get professional medical help, the better. It might take some time, but that time is well spent helping you manage your anxiety and feel your best.

COMMON SYMPTOMS OF ANXIETY

Anxiety can show up in a variety of ways, and understanding its symptoms can help you recognize and cope with what you may experience. Here are some common symptoms that often accompany different types of anxiety:

Generalized Anxiety Disorder (GAD)

Excessive Worry: Imagine having a worry soundtrack that never stops playing. Teens with GAD often find themselves overthinking and stressing about everyday situations, even when there's no apparent reason for concern.

Physical Tension: GAD can cause muscle tension, making your body feel tight and uncomfortable, and can even make it difficult to sleep. You may also experience phantom pains in different parts of your body or stomach that are unrelated to any physical conditions.

Social Anxiety

Nervousness in Social Situations: Ever felt like all eyes were on you? This type of anxiety can make socializing challenging, accompanied by intense feelings of self-consciousness and nervousness.

Avoidance: Teens with social anxiety may avoid social situations altogether to prevent feelings of discomfort. They steer clear of interacting with people or environments where they are surrounded by people.

Panic Attacks

Sudden Intense Fear: Picture a sudden thunderstorm on a clear day. Panic attacks can hit like lightning, causing an overwhelming surge of fear, rapid heartbeat, and difficulty breathing. It might feel like you are suffocating.

Feeling Out of Control: Imagine being in the passenger's seat during a high-speed chase with no way to reach the brakes. Panic attacks can leave teens feeling like they've lost control over their own bodies.

Obsessive-Compulsive Disorder (OCD)

Intrusive Thoughts: Try to visualize a sticky note on your brain that won't go away. OCD can bring persistent, unwanted thoughts that are difficult or impossible to shake.

Compulsive Behaviors: These are like trying to solve a puzzle that never ends. Teens with OCD may feel compelled to perform certain rituals or behaviors to alleviate anxiety, even if they know the behaviors are irrational.

Post-Traumatic Stress Disorder (PTSD)

Flashbacks: Ever have to watch a horror movie you didn't choose? PTSD can bring vivid and distressing memories of a traumatic event, bringing those feelings to the surface and making it feel like the past is happening in the present.

Hypervigilance: Imagine having a radar that's always on. PTSD can heighten alertness and sensitivity to potential threats, leading to a constant state of tension.

Nightmares: The nightmares triggered by PTSD sometimes involve the initial trauma, but other times they may seem entirely unrelated.

Separation Anxiety

Fear of Being Alone: This fear is like losing your way, alone, in a vast forest. Separation anxiety can make teens fear being away from loved ones, leading to anxiety when faced with separation, even if the separation is temporary. It can appear as feeling as if something is wrong or not safe when you are away from people you care about, even when there is evidence everything is fine.

Physical Symptoms: Just like a storm brewing, separation anxiety can bring physical symptoms like stomachaches, headaches, or nausea when even thinking about being apart from the people who make you feel safe.

Specific Phobias

Intense Fear: Imagine encountering a monster under your bed. Specific phobias can trigger an intense, irrational fear response to a particular object or situation.

Avoidance: Teens with specific phobias may go to great lengths to avoid the source of their fear. Imagine wanting to avoid crowds, so you never go grocery shopping; fearing a car accident, so you never learn how to drive, or having a fear of rejection, so you avoid companionship altogether. These can become debilitating and make functioning hard.

Health Anxiety (Hypochondria)

Excessive Health Concerns: Health anxiety can lead to constant worry about potential illnesses, even when there's no evidence to support these concerns. These fears can even manifest physical symptoms that feel real.

Frequent Doctor Visits: Teens with health anxiety may find themselves making frequent trips to the doctor, seeking reassurance about their health status.

ANXIETY'S AFFECT
ON THE MIND
AND BODY

Let's dive into how anxiety plays tricks on both your mind and body. Understanding its shenanigans can be your secret weapon to reclaim control.

Mind

Overthinking and Racing Thoughts: Ever had a million thoughts buzzing around in your brain, making it feel like a crowded party? Anxiety cranks that up to eleven. It's like having a playlist of worries on repeat, making it tough to focus on anything else.

Trouble Concentrating: Imagine trying to read a book while someone is blasting music. Anxiety can make it hard to concentrate, making even simple tasks feel like climbing a mental mountain. It can even cause what is commonly referred to as "brain fog" where thoughts become muddled, disconnected, and difficult to express.

Feeling on Edge: This is like standing on the edge of a cliff, always anticipating something. Anxiety can leave you feeling jittery and restless like you're constantly waiting for something to go wrong.

Negative Thinking: Picture wearing glasses that only see the gloomy side of things. Anxiety can tint your perspective, making it easy to see the negatives and miss the positives. There are different levels of intensity to negative thinking. Often when people mention "spiraling" when it comes to negative thoughts, it means getting caught in a mental loop of possible bad outcomes. Sometimes, this can even get to the point where imaginary bad outcomes start to feel like the truth or real.

Difficulty Making Decisions: Anxiety can make decision-making feel overwhelming, turning even the smallest choices into a mental tug-of-war. This can even lead to "decision paralysis" where it feels like you are physically unable to take any actions at all. It can often occur with small, everyday decisions like deciding what to eat or wear, as well as bigger choices.

Body

Racing Heart: Anxiety can make it feel like your heart is trying to break a speed record. It can send your heart into overdrive, making it pound like you just saw a ghost.

Shortness of Breath: Anxiety can make your breaths shallow and quick as if you're running a marathon even when you're just sitting still. This can even get to the point where it feels as if you can't breathe at all.

Upset Stomach: Anxiety can cause nausea, stomachaches, and that fluttery feeling like a butterfly colony has set up shop inside your gut.

Muscle Tension: Anxiety can tense up your muscles, leaving you feeling as tight and sore as if you'd just finished an intense workout.

Sweating: Anxiety can lead to sweaty palms, damp foreheads, and other unexpected perspiration, even when you're sitting in a cool room.

Understanding how anxiety affects your mind and body can help you navigate these challenges. If you notice these symptoms, don't worry—you're not alone, and help is available. But be aware: Sometimes anxiety doesn't neatly fit into these symptom categories. It's like an unpredictable puzzle with pieces that change shape. You might feel uneasy, experience random worries, or face moments of discomfort without a clear cause. This is why professional help is such a vital part of managing symptoms.

Over time, as you become more familiar with your emotions, you'll recognize these subtle signs—the quiet whispers of anxiety that don't always fit the textbook definitions. Trust your instincts, tune into your feelings, and remember that understanding your unique anxiety language is a journey. With time and self-awareness, you'll become an expert at deciphering the nuanced signals your mind and body send your way.

HEALTHY AND UNHEALTHY ANXIETY

Anxiety is not a one-size-fits-all emotion; there are healthy and unhealthy types of anxiety. Some types give you a boost, like the jittery feeling before a date, while others might be nearly disabling, leaving you unable to step outside your house. Let's take a look at the different sides of anxiety and learn to distinguish between the good and not-so-good vibes.

Healthy Anxiety

Motivation Boost: Healthy anxiety is like having a personal cheerleader in your corner. It nudges you to get stuff done, propelling you to study for that exam or prepare for that presentation. It's the little push that says, "You got this!"

Alertness: Picture a superhero sense tingling when danger is near. Healthy anxiety heightens your senses, making you more alert and ready to tackle challenges. It's your body's way of saying, "Stay sharp!"

Problem-Solving Power: Sometimes anxiety activates your brain's superhero mode. Healthy anxiety helps you think on your feet, coming up with creative solutions when faced with obstacles. It's the spark that turns challenges into opportunities.

Preparation: Healthy anxiety is the friend who reminds you to pack an umbrella when clouds gather. It encourages you to be prepared for what might come, whether it's a school project or a social event. It's your brain saying, "Better safe than sorry!"

Unhealthy Anxiety

Overwhelming Worry: Unhealthy anxiety can have you drowning in worries that don't match the situation. It's a constant nagging that keeps you up at night and prevents you from enjoying the moment.

Physical Distress: Unhealthy anxiety can cause physical symptoms like headaches, stomachaches, and muscle tension, often without a clear reason.

Avoidance: Picture a fence that keeps you from adventures. Unhealthy anxiety might make you dodge situations or people, creating barriers to new experiences. It's the fear that holds you back, whispering, "It's dangerous out there!"

Perfectionism: This is like aiming for a bullseye but never feeling satisfied. Unhealthy anxiety can drive you to set unrealistic standards, making you feel like you're never quite good enough. It's the relentless pursuit of flawlessness that can lead to burnout and sometimes keeps you from even trying.

How to Spot the Difference:

Intensity: Ask yourself, "Is my anxiety proportionate to the situation?" Healthy anxiety feels like a gentle nudge, while unhealthy anxiety is more like a rough shove.

Impact on Daily Life: Consider whether anxiety is helping or hindering your daily activities. Healthy anxiety motivates; unhealthy anxiety disrupts and overwhelms.

Duration: Healthy anxiety is often short-lived, providing a burst of energy or clarity. Unhealthy anxiety lingers, becoming a constant companion rather than a temporary ally.

Awareness: Think about whether your anxiety is based on realistic concerns or irrational fears. Healthy anxiety is grounded in reality, while unhealthy anxiety may be fueled by unwarranted worries.

Activity: Draw or paint a picture of how anxiety makes you feel.

CHAPTER THREE: MANAGING ANXIETY THROUGH SELF-CARE

SELF-CARE AND ANXIETY MANAGEMENT

We've all had those moments where anxiety tries to squeeze into the driver's seat of our lives. But guess what? You've got the ultimate toolkit to keep that anxiety in check — it's called self-care. In the chaos of assignments, social drama, and the constant buzz of teenage life, taking care of yourself might feel like a low priority. But here's the truth: Self-care is your secret weapon against the anxiety monster. Let's break down why it's crucial for managing anxiety and how you can turn self-care into your own personal superhero.

You Deserve It

Hey, you're important! Self-care isn't a luxury; it's a necessity. Taking care of yourself will make it easier to manage unwanted symptoms. They can help you cope and function to the best of your ability.

It's Not Selfish — It's Smart

Self-care isn't about being selfish; it's about being smart. Think of it like charging your batteries so you're ready for whatever comes next. Taking care of yourself ensures you're ready to tackle life's twists and turns. It can also help prepare you, so you can show up for the special people in your life. If you are well cared for, you'll have more energy and the mental presence to show up for the important events in your life.

COMPONENTS OF SELF-CARE

We will talk a bit more about these components in a few minutes, but here's a glance at some of the most important self-care treatments that you can implement right now

Recharging with Sleep

You're not a robot; you need sleep! Good rest is like pressing the reset button on your brain. Quality sleep boosts your mood, helps you focus, and keeps you energized for the epic teen journey. Just like your body heals with rest, your mind can too. Often, people suffering from anxiety require more sleep. If you are going through a difficult time, try to head to bed ten hours before you need to wake up, even if you don't sleep the whole time. Complete quiet activities without electronics, such as reading, until you fall asleep. Allotting more time for sleep in your daily schedule will make it easier to get more rest as your body needs it.

Fueling the Brain with Healthy Eating

Food isn't just fuel; it's brainpower! Choosing nutritious meals gives your brain the energy it needs to navigate the highs and lows of teenage life.

Exercise — The Mood Booster

Exercise releases happy chemicals in your brain, making you feel better. Plus, it's a fantastic stressbuster!

Chill Time with Relaxation Techniques

When life gets hectic, take advantage of relaxation techniques. Whether it's deep breaths, meditation, or finding a quiet spot to recharge, these are your go-to moves to dial down the stress.

MAKING SELF-CARE A PRIORITY

Start Small

You don't have to overhaul your life. Begin with small, manageable steps. Maybe it's setting a consistent sleep schedule, trying a new recipe, or going for a walk.

Find What Works for You

Self-care is personal. Experiment with different activities until you find what clicks. Whether it's journaling, playing an instrument, or simply enjoying nature, find what lights you up, refreshes you, and calms you.

Make it Routine

Turn self-care into a habit. Schedule it into your day, just like you would homework or hanging out with friends. Consistency is key to reaping the full benefits.

Wrapping It Up

Managing anxiety can seem impossible, but self-care is the key to making it achievable. You've got the tools—sleep, healthy eating, exercise, and relaxation techniques—to make anxiety say "I'm outta here!"

GETTING ENOUGH SLEEP

First, let's talk about something we all need more of but often struggle to get—sleep! Between school, socializing, and those endless screen sessions, catching enough Z's might feel like an elusive goal. In your teen years, it is more tempting to skip out on sleep like your peers. However, a lack of sleep will intensify your symptoms, making it harder to function. But fear not, we've got some practical tips to help you snag the sleep your body and mind crave.

Set a Consistent Schedule

Your body loves routine, and setting a consistent sleep schedule is like giving it a comforting bedtime story. Try going to bed and waking up at the same time every day, even on weekends. This helps regulate your internal clock, making it easier to fall asleep and wake up naturally.

Create a Sleep-Inducing Environment

Make your bedroom a sleep haven. Keep it cool, dark, and quiet. Consider using blackout curtains, earplugs, or a white noise machine if needed. Try not to do anything but sleep in your bed; your sleep environment should signal to your brain that it's time to wind down.

Limit Screen Time Before Bed

We know, we know—scrolling through your phone or binge-watching your favorite shows is tempting. However, the blue light emitted by screens can mess with your body's production of the sleep hormone melatonin. Try to power down at least an hour before bedtime. If you must use screens, use blue light filters.

Be Mindful of What You Eat and Drink

Your bedtime snacks can impact your sleep. Avoid heavy, rich meals close to bedtime, and be cautious with caffeine and nicotine. These stimulants can interfere with your ability to fall asleep. Opt for a light snack if you're hungry before bed.

Get Moving During the Day

Regular exercise can act like a pressure valve for your body. Engaging in physical activity helps regulate your sleep patterns and promotes a more restful slumber. Aim for at least 30 minutes of moderate exercise most days but try not to squeeze in a workout right before bedtime.

Wind Down with Relaxation Techniques

Create a pre-sleep routine that signals to your body that it's time to wind down. This could include activities like reading a book, taking a warm bath, or practicing relaxation techniques like deep breathing. These rituals help transition your mind from the hustle of the day to a more relaxed state.

Limit Naps

Power naps are great, but lengthy siestas during the day can mess with your nighttime sleep. If you need a nap, keep it short (around 20-30 minutes) and earlier in the day to avoid interfering with your bedtime routine.

Listen to Your Body

Finally, tune in to what your body is telling you. If you're consistently tired during the day, it's a sign that you probably need more sleep. Don't ignore these signals; prioritize your well-being and adjust your sleep habits accordingly. Your peers may get by on little sleep, but for people prone to anxiety, a lack of sleep will make it harder to function. If you are irritable, experiencing "brain fog," have increased negative thoughts, or are feeling jittery, you should try your best to get ten hours of sleep.

If you are skeptical, start keeping notes on your phone. Whenever you remember to, write down how many hours of sleep you got, what symptoms you experienced, and their intensity level on a scale of 1-10. You'll start to notice patterns regarding how much sleep your body needs during "normal" times versus higher stress periods.

Getting more sleep is a game-changer, and implementing these tips can pave the way for more restful nights. Quality sleep is a crucial ingredient for overall well-being and will help keep anxiety at bay. You deserve to wake up feeling refreshed and ready to tackle the day ahead.

HEALTHY EATING

In this section, we'll take a deeper look into the world of healthy eating, which works with regular exercise to create a dynamic duo that keeps your body and mind in top-notch shape. We get it; amidst the school craziness, social whirlwinds, and fast food, it's easy to feel like maintaining a healthy lifestyle is a challenge. Don't worry—we've got some practical strategies to help you make nutritious choices and stay active without breaking a sweat (well, maybe just a little).

Balance is Key

Picture your plate as a canvas and aim for a colorful masterpiece. Include a variety of fruits, vegetables, whole grains, and lean proteins in your meals. This ensures you get a mix of essential nutrients for a healthy and balanced diet. If you prefer snacking, try to snack on a handful of healthy food at consistent intervals. Remember, sweets are okay as long as they are portioned and accompanied by healthy food. The fuller you are and the more nutrients you get during the day, the less cravings you'll experience for unhealthy foods. It's also a good idea to keep ahead of your hunger. If you allow yourself to get "hangry," you will find it much more difficult to handle your symptoms.

Snack Smart

Snacking doesn't have to be the enemy! Choose nutrient-dense snacks like fruits, veggies, nuts, hard-boiled eggs, pickles, or yogurt. Avoid mindlessly munching on processed snacks; instead, opt for whole foods that keep you energized without the post-snack guilt. Portioning out your food before eating can help keep you from overindulging.

Stay Hydrated

Water is your best friend. Not only does it keep you hydrated, but it also supports overall well-being. Carry a water bottle with you throughout the day and aim to drink plenty of H2O. It's a simple yet powerful step for maintaining good health. Dehydration can increase anxiety symptoms.

Plan and Prep

Planning your meals and snacks ahead of time gives you a roadmap for healthy eating. Take a moment to think about what you'll eat during the day and consider prepping snacks or meals in advance to avoid reaching for less-nutritious options when hunger strikes. You can also think ahead further toward events where you know unhealthy foods will be served. By keeping these in mind, you can use them to motivate you to eat healthier leading up to and following the special event.

Mindful Eating

Slow down and savor your food. Mindful eating turns a meal into a meditation session. Pay attention to flavors, textures, and your body's hunger and fullness cues. Doing so helps you enjoy your food more and prevents overeating.

THE POWER OF EXERCISING

As mentioned above, exercising can help boost your mood, improve your sleep, act as a coping mechanism, and aid in symptom management. Most people think of exercise as running long periods or lifting weights, but the truth is that there are a lot of fun physical activities that don't feel like work.

Although you should try to fit in 30-45 minutes of exercise that elevates your heartbeat, you don't have to do it in one continuous block. Completing short bursts of exercise can have just as many effects as one long session. The key is to increase your physical activity and try to make it a part of your daily life. To do this, you'll have to try many combinations of different techniques and activities until you find what works best for you personally.

Find Activities You Enjoy

Exercise doesn't have to be a chore; it can be an adventure! Explore different activities until you find something you genuinely enjoy — whether it's dancing, hiking, playing a sport, or even just going for a brisk walk. When exercise is fun, you're more likely to stick with it. Make a list of everything physical you know you have fun doing and then list out some activities that you are interested in trying. There are video tutorials online, community classes, and school teams that can help you discover new, fun, physical activities.

Mix it Up

Variety is the spice of life, and the same goes for your workouts. Mix up your exercise routine to keep things interesting and target different muscle groups. This can prevent boredom and ensure you're getting a well-rounded fitness experience. Maybe you go on a short walk between classes, take a bike ride with some friends, dance while you are cleaning your room, complete some sets of push-ups on your study break, or stretch out while watching a movie. The more activities you incorporate into your daily routine, the easier it will be to get adequate exercise. Some days, you might need to take it easier than others. It's a good idea to have a handful of "easy" and relaxing exercises for more difficult days.

Make it Social

Turn exercise into a social event by working out with friends or joining group classes. This helps combine fun with fitness. Having a workout buddy not only adds accountability but also makes the whole experience more enjoyable. If you don't want the commitment or pressure of a workout buddy, that's okay! You can still ask friends to join you on a walk or get people together for a game like frisbee golf.

Set Realistic Goals

Instead of aiming for the moon, set achievable fitness goals. Whether it's increasing your daily step count, improving your flexibility, or trying a new workout routine, setting realistic goals helps you stay motivated and track your progress. It's recommended to start by listing out all of the activities you know you enjoy doing and find ways to add in one at a time. Start with something small like yoga in the morning or an afternoon walk. Once this feels natural, add on another habit. Remember, some days you'll feel like doing less, and some days you'll have the motivation to do more. Take advantage of the days you feel up for more and don't beat yourself up on the harder days.

Incorporate Exercise into Your Routine

Turn everyday activities into opportunities for movement. This was mentioned above, but it's worth repeating. Walk or bike to school, take the stairs instead of the elevator, or have a dance party in your room. Small, consistent efforts add up and contribute to an active lifestyle. It's sometimes easier to fit in 5 minutes of strength training or cardio, multiple times throughout the day than it is to find the time for 30-45 minutes at once.

Committing to eating healthy and exercising regularly might sound like a big ask, but these strategies are all about making it practical and enjoyable. You're not aiming for perfection; you're aiming for progress. It's vital to make choices that nourish our bodies and keep us moving with the energy and vitality of unstoppable teens!

RELAXATION TECHNIQUES

As you know, life can throw some crazy curveballs our way, and it's totally okay to feel a bit overwhelmed sometimes. That's where relaxation techniques come in. Think of them as your secret weapons against stress and anxiety. Below are a few relaxation techniques, but there are many, many other options out there. Ideally, you want your mind and body working on something completely different than your daily worries. The best relaxation techniques combine mental stimulation with a physical component. These are helpful to use when you are particularly stressed as well as part of your daily self-care routines.

Deep Breathing

When stressed, one of the first and easiest ways to help calm your nervous system is with breathing techniques. The simplest form is simply deep breaths. Inhale into your belly, filling your stomach and chest with as much air as possible. Hold it for a second or two, and then release it slowly. Repeat this until your muscles start to relax.

You can also use timed breathing patterns, which require you to focus your mind on the task and can help distract you from racing thoughts. The first is square breathing. Inhale for a count of four, exhale for a count of four and then repeat. The second is known as the 4-7-8 method. Inhale for a count of four, hold your breath for a count of seven and exhale for a count of eight. This is a good relaxation technique when you don't have a lot of time or privacy available.

Another method is to trace your hand with your opposite index finger as you breathe. Inhale as you trace up your thumb, exhale as you trace down, and continue the process for each finger. When you reach your pinky, repeat the process back until you reach your thumb again.

Massage

Although you most likely don't have access to a professional massage therapist, you can still massage various body parts. Often, we store tension and stress in our muscles. Working some of these muscle groups out can help ease our minds. First, focus on breathing into the areas that are creating discomfort. Then apply pressure with your hands and rub the muscles in small circular motions. If you have the time, try starting at the bottom of your feet and slowly moving up your body, paying special attention to areas like your arches, calves, shoulders, and neck where tension tends to amplify. You can also ask a friend or loved one to help you with this when it's possible and comfortable to do so.

Yoga

Yoga is a particularly helpful form of relaxation because it combines physical movement with breathwork. There are many free resources available online in the form of infographics, videos, and articles. There are also books, streaming options, and DVDs that you can acquire to help guide your practice. The most important part is to align your breathing with the activity. There are certain points where you inhale while completing a move and exhale as you're changing positions. This requires your full attention and helps increase the amount of oxygen within your bloodstream.

Music

If you are stressed out, you can try putting on headphones and playing your favorite songs. They don't even have to be happy songs. Sometimes, playing sad music when you're sad can help you cry and release the emotion from your body. Likewise, angry music while upset could give you a way to outlet the feelings inside. If possible, try dancing and singing with the music. The more physical you are, the more endorphins are released which can help with your mood.

Artwork

You don't need to be good at art to use it as a form of relaxation. In fact, simply drawing repeated shapes in colors that match your mood can work to help pull you out of your head and get you focused on something else. For example, let's say you are feeling extremely worried about a test and keep thinking about it, even though you've done everything you can to prepare for it.

Try taking out a piece of paper and drawing circles. At first, the circles might come out as fervent scribbles, but eventually, your mind will start to space out and the action become somewhat mindless. This is a good thing. You'll be able to tell when you are calm. This can also be achieved by filling in a coloring book or painting layers of colors you find alluring. The only rule is not to worry about the outcome. This isn't for anyone else's eyes. If by chance you are decent at drawing or painting, use this talent to create something meaningful to you. The more meticulous and repetitive the actions, the better. You want your mind to go blank and your body to move without judgment.

Aromatherapy

Essential oils are quite popular these days, but there are other ways to incorporate aromatherapy. Sure, if you have an oil burner, a favorite candle, or incense, go ahead and use them. Scents such as lavender have a proven calming effect. If you don't, though, that's okay. There are other smells that will naturally relax you. For example, the smell of baking cookies usually has a positive effect on most people. You might need to get a little creative with this one but pay attention to what smells feel comforting. Dryer sheets, tea, coffee, and certain bath products are other common smells that put people at ease. Our minds tend to connect memories and smells together. A scent can trigger nostalgic feelings and be a useful tool in calming yourself.

Healthy Distraction

Distraction is another relaxation method that can prove to be helpful when done in moderation. The goal here is to avoid activities that can trigger additional stress or become completely mind-numbing. Scrolling social media pages is not a good choice. Neither are games that are designed without goals (think of all of those gem-crushing and matching games). If you want to play a game, select one that has a storyline and brings real excitement and focus. You should choose one that will require your full attention. You shouldn't be able to win a level while also stressing about your upcoming tests and talking to a sibling. Same thing with television. Instead of watching a show you can mindlessly binge without paying close attention, choose a movie that requires your full investment. Maybe even select one in a foreign language that requires you to read, listen, and watch all at once. Another idea is to pair an audiobook or podcast with an activity that uses your hands such as knitting, crocheting, building a model, or completing a puzzle.

CREATING RELAXING DAILY HABITS

Start with Short Sessions

You don't need to do anything for hours. Begin with short relaxation sessions, maybe 5-10 minutes, and gradually increase as you become more comfortable. Consistency is key.

Explore Different Techniques

There's no one-size-fits-all when it comes to relaxation. Explore different techniques — deep breathing, guided imagery, progressive muscle relaxation — and find what resonates with you. You can look online or ask someone you respect for more ideas.

Incorporate Them into Your Routine

Make relaxation techniques a part of your daily routine. Whether it's before bedtime, during a study break, or when you wake up, find a time that works for you. Consistency helps these techniques become a natural and beneficial part of your day. If you do them regularly, then you are more likely to remember them as options when you really need them.

Activity: Practice deep breathing for five minutes.

CHAPTER FOUR:
BUILDING RESILIENCE

WHAT IS RESILIENCE?

Dealing with anxiety is like gearing up for a wild adventure—you won't dodge all the bumps, but you can put together a mental toolkit that'll help you handle the twists and turns. For teens, it's vital to get the lowdown on resilience, which is basically the power to bounce back when life throws challenges our way.

Think of resilience as a mental muscle that gets stronger over time. It's not about dodging stress, but learning how to handle it like a pro. It's like upgrading your game when facing challenges, not avoiding them.

Resilience is about thinking tough, talking it out, setting achievable goals, staying in the moment, and taking care of your mind and body. With these moves, you're not just surviving—you're owning the game of teenage life.

In some circles, resilience is referred to as a window of tolerance. As we get older, we learn how to tolerate more and more hardships without breaking down. Think about when you were younger. At one point, it was extremely frustrating not being able to walk. You'd fall down, possibly cry, stand back up, and try again. Eventually, falling down isn't scary or a concern. You start walking and even when you trip or stumble, you just keep going unbothered.

Think about the aspects of life that once were difficult but now feel easy to you. Resilience to stress is extremely similar. We can't completely avoid stress, but we can increase our tolerance to stressful situations as well as improve how fast we bounce back afterward.

STRATEGIES FOR BUILDING RESILIENCE

Resilience isn't just something you're just born with. You can build resilience over time, just like any other muscle. This section talks about some real-life strategies to boost your resilience game and handle whatever comes your way.

Growth Mindset

Think of challenges as puzzles, not roadblocks. Resilience is about seeing setbacks as opportunities to grow smarter and stronger. Embrace the idea that every hiccup is a chance to level up in the game of life. Instead of focusing on winning or achieving, focus on trying your best and improving.

Communication

Communication is one key to bouncing back from failures because it can help you learn that things aren't as bad as you think. Open up to your squad—friends, family, or professionals. Life's a team sport, and sharing your thoughts and feelings isn't a sign of weakness; it's a strength. You're not alone and letting others in on your journey can make a huge difference.

Goal Setting

Set some goals but keep it real. Resilience involves breaking down big dreams into achievable steps. This isn't about overwhelming yourself; it's about celebrating the small victories along the way. Those tiny wins add up, and before you know it, you've conquered the big stuff.

Mindfulness

Mindfulness is like a mental workout. Instead of stressing about what's already happened or freaking out about what might come, focus on the now. Practice deep breathing, meditation, or quick mindfulness exercises. There is also a common saying "Focus on your hands and feet." This means focusing physically on what is right in front of you in that moment. Maybe you can't do anything about what is worrying you, but you can clean your room, go on a walk, or complete an art project and focus your full attention on that. These techniques are not about escaping reality; they're about powering up your calm and focus levels.

Lifestyle Choices

Now, let's talk lifestyle. Treat your body right, and it'll treat you right. Exercise regularly, eat a balanced diet, and get enough sleep. These aren't just clichés; they're the keys to unlocking your full potential. A healthy body supports a healthy mind, and together, they make you unstoppable.

Accepting Change

Building resilience is also about adapting to change. Life doesn't follow a script, and that's okay. Flexibility is your ally. Learn to roll with the punches, adjust your plans when needed, and embrace the unexpected. It's not about having all the answers; it's about learning how to find them.

Laugh

Here's a secret weapon: laughter. Find joy in the little things, share a laugh with friends, and don't take everything too seriously. Laughter isn't just good for the soul; it's a powerful tool in your resilience toolkit.

In a nutshell, resilience is your ultimate life skill. It's about thinking big, talking it out, setting realistic goals, staying present, celebrating victories, taking care of your body, adapting to change, and laughing along the way.

BOUNCING BACK FROM SETBACKS

Let's face it: setbacks are going to happen—but fear not! Bouncing back is a skill you can totally master. Here's your guide on how to shake off setbacks and come back stronger than ever.

Perspective

When you hit a bump in the road, try seeing it as a detour rather than a dead end. Life rarely goes as planned, and setbacks are just part of the journey. Embrace the idea that these twists and turns are opportunities for growth and learning.

Emotions

Next up, let's talk about feelings. It's totally okay to feel upset, frustrated, or disappointed when things don't go your way. Acknowledge those emotions instead of pushing them aside. Vent to a friend, write in a journal or just take a moment to reflect. Processing your emotions is a crucial step in building resilience.

Avoid Blaming

Resist the urge to play the blame game. Whether it's your fault or not, dwelling on or assigning guilt won't change the situation. Instead, focus on what you can control: your response. Take responsibility for your part, learn from it, and use that knowledge to make better choices in the future.

Seeking Support

Support is crucial. Lean on your friends, family, or mentors when you're facing difficulties. They're there to offer guidance, encouragement, and sometimes just a sympathetic ear. You're not alone in this journey, and seeking support is a sign of strength, not weakness.

Remember, setbacks don't define you. One bad day, mishap, or even the occasional failure doesn't erase your achievements or potential. Learn from mistakes, but don't let them overshadow your progress and resilience.

Lastly, have faith in yourself. Trust that you have the strength to overcome challenges. You've bounced back before, and you'll do it again. Believe in your abilities, stay positive, and keep moving forward.

LEARNING FROM MISTAKES

Everyone is familiar with making mistakes. The good news is that making mistakes is a completely normal part of life. The best part? You can turn those slip-ups into powerful lessons. Here are the facts on why and how to learn from your mistakes.

First off, no one's perfect, not your BFF, not your favorite celebrity, not even that one person who seems to have it all together. We all mess up because, hey, we're human, so cut yourself some slack. Making mistakes doesn't mean you're a failure; it means you're living, learning, and growing.

Now, let's dig into why mistakes are actually a secret weapon for conquering anxiety. Think of them as road signs on the journey of life. They're pointing out where you might need to make a turn or a detour. Mistakes highlight areas for improvement, and every slip-up is a chance to get better at this game called life. Below are a few of the values that can be practiced through mistakes.

Responsibility

One crucial lesson from mistakes is responsibility. Making mistakes provides the opportunity to own up to your blunders. It's tempting to blame others or the universe when things go wrong, but taking responsibility is the first step toward growth. Whether it's a small hiccup or a major mess, acknowledging your role is like unlocking a door to self-improvement.

Accountability

Now let's talk about the "A" word—accountability. It's not just about saying, "Yep, I messed up." It's about figuring out why it happened and how you can avoid a repeat performance. This isn't about dwelling on the past, but about creating a smarter future version of yourself.

Problem-Solving

Now, here's the fun part—problem-solving. Every mistake is a riddle waiting to be solved. What went wrong, and how can you fix it? Put your detective hat on and start finding solutions. This process sharpens your problem-solving skills, and trust us, that's a big deal in the real world.

Resilience

Next up, is resilience. Yep, there's that word again. Ever heard the phrase "fall down seven times, get up eight"? Learning from mistakes builds your comeback muscles. It's not about avoiding the fall; it's about getting back on your feet stronger and wiser.

Gratitude

Now, let's flip the script and talk about gratitude. You read that right: Mistakes can teach you to appreciate the good stuff. When you mess up, understanding the mistake can often help to shine a spotlight on what you value and what really matters to you. It's important to be grateful for the lessons, even if they come in disguise.

Self-Awareness

Mistakes are also a lesson in self-awareness. Understanding why you made a particular blunder gives you insight into yourself. It's a journey of self-discovery, and the more you know about yourself, the better equipped you are for the twists and turns of life.

Mistakes aren't the end of the world — they're your training ground for success. Embrace them! Life's an epic adventure and learning from your mistakes is your roadmap to becoming the awesome person you're meant to be.

Activity: Write down one thing you have learned from a difficult experience.

CHAPTER FIVE: DEVELOPING A POSITIVE MINDSET

It's tough being a teenager. Between school, social drama, and the looming future, it's easy to feel overwhelmed. But guess what? You've got a secret weapon against all that stress: positive thinking. Let's examine how this mindset can be your ultimate ally in conquering anxiety.

WHAT'S "POSITIVE THINKING"?

Positive thinking isn't about pretending everything's perfect. It's more about finding a silver lining even in the stormiest situations. Instead of letting negativity take over, positive thinking empowers you to transform setbacks into opportunities for growth. It's your ally for navigating the twists and turns of teenage life with confidence, reminding you that you've got the strength to rise above any challenge. So, buckle up and embrace the power of positive thinking—your mind's reliable companion is ready for action!

Keep in mind that positive thinking isn't just for the teenage years—it's a lifelong asset that will pay off big time in adulthood. Cultivating a positive mindset now sets the stage for resilience and adaptability as you face the unpredictable challenges of grown-up life. Positive thinking provides a strategy for handling stress, fostering healthier relationships, and approaching career goals with confidence. By embracing positivity early on, you're not just navigating teenage tribulations; you're investing in a mindset that will serve you well as you navigate the adult journey ahead. By shifting to a more positive mindset, you are more likely to succeed in many areas as well as lower your stress level.

STRATEGIES FOR POSITIVE THINKING

Deflecting Anxiety with Positivity

Sometimes our mind compulsively generates negative thoughts. One way we can start to re-write these patterns is by thinking three positive thoughts to counteract the negative one. This can feel somewhat corny and awkward at first. One easy way to practice this is to list three things you are grateful for. For example, you might have a negative thought about your math class. An example of correcting this with positivity might be to think, *I am grateful: I have time to practice, that there are tutors and resources at school to help me learn the material, and that this math class and my current skill level are only a temporary situation.* You won't catch every negative thought and that's okay. Just do what you can, when you can to correct them.

Gratitude Journaling

As mentioned above, gratitude is helpful. It aids in shifting your perspective from what you lack to what you already have in your life. A gratitude journal will increase your awareness and daily focus on what's good in your life. Start a gratitude journal by jotting down three things you're thankful for every day. It could be as simple as a sunny day, a compliment from a friend, or a delicious meal. Some days this will feel forced or awkward, and that's normal. Just keep at it, and you'll notice that it becomes second nature.

Positive Affirmations

Create a list of positive affirmations that resonate with you. These are short, uplifting statements that you can repeat daily. It might feel a bit strange at first, but affirmations can reshape your thoughts and boost your confidence. For example, tell yourself, "I am capable of overcoming challenges," and watch your self-confidence grow.

Surround Yourself with Positivity

Surround yourself with people who uplift and support you. Evaluate your circle of friends and influences. Positive vibes are contagious, and being around friends who share a constructive outlook can have a significant impact on your own mindset. You can also surround yourself with positivity by decorating your room and spaces with images and phrases that feel good. Spend some extra time making your living area aesthetically pleasing, comforting, and relaxing. Another idea is to write inspiring quotes on sticky notes and leave them in places you look often such as your desk or bathroom mirror.

Limit Negative Media Consumption

Be mindful of what you consume through social media, news, and other platforms. Too much negativity can impact your mindset. Try to balance your media diet with positive and uplifting content. Unfollow accounts that bring you down and seek out sources that inspire and motivate. Next, take a good look at your social media pages and analyze what your algorithm is bringing to your feed. You can request that certain posts don't show up by adjusting your settings. Likewise, you can change what pops up on your page by intentionally interacting with pages and posts that bring you joy. Try to fill your feed up with hobbies, inspiration, knowledge, and humor rather than what's going on with other people.

Volunteer and Help Others

Engaging in acts of kindness and volunteering not only makes a positive impact on others but also boosts your own sense of well-being. It provides a different perspective on life and reinforces the idea that positivity can be a force for good in the world. You can find volunteer opportunities by talking to instructors at your school, asking your family, or searching online. Volunteer work doesn't need to be formal, either. Simply ask your family and friends how you can help.

Remember, building a positive mindset is a journey, not a destination. It takes time and practice, so be patient with yourself. These strategies are powerful tools in your mental arsenal—use them consistently and watch how they shape your outlook on life.

CHALLENGING NEGATIVE THOUGHTS

Sometimes it might feel like the pieces of life don't quite fit together. One major challenge is those pesky negative thoughts that sneak in and cloud your mind. The good news? You've got the power to challenge and change them! Here's your guide to mastering this mental game and reshaping the way you think.

Identify Negative Thoughts

First things first—in order to challenge your negative thoughts, you've got to recognize them when they pop up. Whether it's self-doubt, fear, or a gloomy outlook, be aware of the thoughts that bring you down. Recognizing negative thoughts takes practice, but it's the first step to retraining your thinking patterns.

Question the Evidence

Often, our minds play tricks on us, blowing things out of proportion. Challenge the validity of your negative thoughts by examining the facts. Ask yourself, "Is there real evidence to support this negative thought?" Are they as bad as they seem, or is your mind exaggerating the situation?

Consider Alternatives

Explore alternative perspectives. Is there another way to interpret the situation? Are there positive aspects you might be overlooking? This step helps you break free from the tunnel vision of negativity and opens your mind to different, more uplifting possibilities.

Challenge Extremes

Avoid falling into the trap of all-or-nothing thinking. Life is rarely black and white. Instead of thinking in extremes, consider the shades of gray. For example, instead of saying, "I totally failed," recognize the effort you put in, the parts you did well, and the progress you've made. Small victories count, so celebrate them!

Practice Self-Compassion

Be kind to yourself. Imagine you're talking to a friend going through the same situation. What words of encouragement would you offer? Treat yourself with the same kindness and understanding. Remember, everyone makes mistakes, and setbacks are a natural part of life.

Challenge Overgeneralization

Avoid making sweeping conclusions based on isolated incidents. Just because one thing went wrong doesn't mean everything will. Challenge thoughts like, "I always mess up" or "Nothing ever goes my way." Recognize that setbacks are specific events, not a never-ending declaration of your inadequacies.

Create a Positive Mantra

Counteract negative thoughts with positive affirmations. Develop a mantra or encouraging statement that resonates with you and repeat it to yourself when negativity creeps in. Over time, these positive reinforcements can become instrumental in shaping your thought patterns.

Seek Support

Share your thoughts with friends, family, or a trusted mentor. They can provide valuable insights, support, and alternative perspectives. Sometimes, an outside viewpoint can offer a fresh angle on challenging situations.

Practice Mindfulness

Engage in mindfulness techniques to stay present and focused. When negative thoughts arise, gently guide your mind back to the present moment. Practices like deep breathing or mindful meditation can help you break free from the cycle of negativity.

Remember that transforming negative thoughts is a skill that improves with practice. You've got the power to reshape your thinking and navigate life's challenges with resilience and positivity. Embrace the journey of self-discovery and turn those mental puzzles into opportunities for growth and empowerment!

PRACTICING GRATITUDE

At times, you might believe that challenging negative thoughts is next to impossible. Well, here's the scoop: You've got a secret key that can make the job a whole lot better—gratitude. It's not just a buzzword; it's a game-changer that can transform your mindset. Let's dive into how making gratitude a habit can shift your outlook from so-so to amazing!

Shifts Focus from What's Lacking to What's Present

When you practice gratitude, you intentionally shift your focus from what's missing in your life to what you already have. Instead of dwelling on what you don't have or what's going wrong, you start noticing and appreciating the positives, no matter how small they might seem.

Fosters a Positive Perspective

Gratitude is like putting on a pair of positivity glasses. It helps you see the good things around you, even in challenging times. This positive perspective can be a game-changer, allowing you to approach situations with a hopeful and optimistic mindset.

Builds Resilience

Life throws curveballs, right? Practicing gratitude is your secret weapon to bounce back. When you focus on the positive aspects of your life, you build resilience. It helps you recover faster from the bad days and moments that are inevitable in life. The practice highlights what is good about a situation, helping make the bad bearable.

Improves Mental Well-being

Gratitude isn't just a warm fuzzy feeling; it's a boost for your mental well-being. Studies show that regularly expressing gratitude can lead to lower levels of stress, anxiety, and depression. It's a natural mood enhancer, making you feel happier and more content.

Strengthens Relationships

Ever notice how expressing gratitude can bring people closer? It's like a friendship glue. When you acknowledge and appreciate people, whether they're friends, family, or even yourself, you strengthen your relationships. This positive energy creates a supportive and uplifting environment.

Encourages a Growth Mindset

Gratitude and a growth mindset go together. When you appreciate the effort you put into overcoming challenges, even if you don't always succeed, you cultivate a mindset that values the process of learning and growing. It's about progress, not perfection.

Boosts Self-Esteem

Practicing gratitude is a confidence booster. When you acknowledge your accomplishments, no matter how small, you start recognizing your own worth. It's a powerful tool for building and maintaining a healthy level of self-esteem.

Creates a Positive Ripple Effect

Gratitude is contagious! When you express appreciation, it often inspires others to do the same. Imagine creating a ripple effect of positivity among your friends, family, and community. It's like spreading sunshine in your social circles.

Enhances Sleep Quality

A positive mindset and good sleep go hand in hand. Gratitude has been linked to improved sleep quality. When you focus on the positive aspects of your life before bedtime, it can help calm your mind, making it easier to drift into a peaceful sleep.

Turns Challenges into Opportunities

Life's full of challenges, but gratitude turns them into opportunities. Instead of seeing setbacks as insurmountable obstacles, gratitude helps you find the lessons and silver linings. It's about facing challenges with a mindset that says, "I've got this!"

How Does Practicing Gratitude Help with Anxiety?

Practicing gratitude shifts your focus from what's stressing you out to what's going well in your life. It's like a mental reset button that helps you appreciate the positives, no matter how small. When you acknowledge and express gratitude, you create a ripple effect of positivity in your mind, gradually easing the grip of anxiety.

Furthermore, gratitude encourages a mindset of abundance rather than scarcity. Instead of dwelling on what you lack or what might go wrong, you start to recognize the abundance of good things around you. This shift in perspective can be a game-changer, reducing the intensity of anxious thoughts and allowing you to navigate challenges with a clearer, more positive mindset.

Practicing gratitude isn't about denying the challenges you face; it's about navigating them with a positive mindset. So, grab your gratitude journal, start counting your blessings, and watch as your outlook on life transforms into a vibrant tapestry of positivity!

Activity: Write down three things you are grateful for.

CHAPTER SIX:
COPING WITH
SOCIAL ANXIETY

WHAT IS
SOCIAL ANXIETY?

Have you ever felt butterflies in your stomach before a party or a presentation? Well, what if we told you there could be more to it than just normal nervousness? Let's dive into the world of social anxiety and figure out what it's all about.

Social Anxiety Is More Than Just Being Shy

Social anxiety isn't just your run-of-the-mill shyness. It's like when you're not just nervous about talking to people, but you're seriously freaking out about being judged or embarrassed. It's a nagging fear that everyone's watching, waiting for you to mess up.

Signs and Symptoms

How do you know if you or someone else is dealing with social anxiety? Well, there are telltale signs. Some of them include: worrying big time before social gatherings, feeling all sweaty and shaky before or while spending time with others, avoiding hangouts or events, nausea experienced before or during social interactions, and always worrying about saying or doing something that'll make you look bad.

First off, pay attention to how you feel before things like parties or presentations. If the very idea of these makes your stomach do gymnastics and you find yourself worrying a ton about what others might think of you, that could be a sign of social anxiety setting up camp. Also, take note if you catch yourself dodging social stuff altogether or feeling like you'd rather face a dragon than hang out with a group. Those avoidance moves might be your brain's way of dealing with social anxiety.

Now, let's talk about the body language of social anxiety. Do you notice your palms getting sweaty, your heart pounding for no apparent reason, or you're constantly fidgeting in social situations? These are like your body dropping hints. Another thing to watch out for is the mental chatter—replaying conversations over and over, worrying about saying the wrong thing or imagining worst-case scenarios—that might be social anxiety knocking on your door. It's all about paying attention to these signs, being kind to yourself, and realizing it's okay to ask for help if you think social anxiety is trying to crash your party.

How Social Anxiety Messes with Your Daily Life

Guess what? Social anxiety isn't just a one-time thing; it can mess with your whole life. Your grades might take a hit because your anxiety makes it hard to focus, making friends becomes a struggle, and you might have intense feelings of loneliness. It's like a dark cloud hanging over everything you do.

This section of our guide will provide you with an in-depth look at social anxiety and give you some helpful strategies for coping when it rears its ugly head.

COMMON TRIGGERS
OF SOCIAL ANXIETY

Triggers for social anxiety can vary from person to person—things like public speaking, starting conversations, or just being in a group can set it off. Parties, school events, or even regular chats can turn into a battle against those anxiety monsters. We're going to explore some of the most common triggers that might make those social butterflies in our stomachs flutter a little too wildly.

Fear of Judgement

Let's face it—we all want to be liked and accepted. The fear of being judged or criticized by our peers is a major trigger for social anxiety. It's natural to worry about how others perceive us, but sometimes this fear can become overwhelming. Thoughts like, "What if they think I'm weird?" or "Am I saying the right thing?" can create mental hurdles that are tough to overcome.

Performance Anxiety

Ever felt like you're putting on a show for the world? Whether it's giving a presentation, performing in a school play, or even just participating in a group discussion, the pressure to perform can be intense. Fear of making a mistake or being the center of attention can trigger social anxiety, making us feel like a spotlight is shining directly on our flaws.

Comparing Ourselves to Others

In the age of social media, it's easy to fall into the comparison trap. Seeing others seemingly living their best lives can make us feel inadequate or like we don't measure up. Constantly comparing ourselves to our peers can intensify social anxiety, making it difficult to appreciate our own unique qualities and achievements.

Difficulty Making Friends

Making friends can be challenging, especially when it feels like everyone else has their own tight-knit circle. The fear of rejection or not being able to connect with others can be a significant trigger for social anxiety. It's essential to remember that building meaningful friendships takes time, and everyone experiences moments of social awkwardness.

Overthinking Social Interactions

We've all been there—replaying conversations in our minds and overthinking every little detail. The fear of saying the wrong thing or not knowing how to respond in social situations can lead to a never-ending loop of anxious thoughts. Learning to let go of perfectionism and embracing the flaws in our interactions are crucial steps in managing social anxiety.

Social Pressures

Whether it's academic expectations, fitting into social cliques, or conforming to societal norms, the pressures placed on teenagers can be overwhelming. Feeling the need to meet certain standards or expectations can contribute to social anxiety, but when the fear of not living up to these ideals looms large, it's important to realize that no one can embody perfection.

Fear of Rejection

Ah, the dreaded fear of rejection—a classic trigger for social anxiety. The idea of putting yourself out there, whether it's asking someone to hang out or expressing our feelings, can be downright scary. The worry about being turned down or not fitting in can make us hesitate to take social risks, keeping us in our comfort zones but also limiting our opportunities for connection and growth.

COPING WITH SOCIAL ANXIETY

We get it; social situations can sometimes feel like a giant maze of awkwardness and nervousness. But fear not! Social anxiety is something many of us face, but effective strategies exist to help you navigate through it.

Deep Breaths for the Win

When anxiety creeps in, your breath becomes your trusty sidekick. Practice deep breathing: Inhale slowly through your nose, hold it for a few seconds, and then exhale through your mouth. Repeat this technique to slow down your racing heart and calm those jitters.

Power Poses: Strike a Confident Stance

Ever heard of power poses? Stand tall, shoulders back and head held high—this could help you feel more self-assured. Confidence isn't just about how you feel; it's about how you present yourself. Striking a power pose might trick your brain into feeling more self-assured.

Script Your Conversations

Worried about running out of things to say? Create a mental script or jot down some talking points before social events. Having a few go-to topics can be like having a cheat code for smooth conversations. Remember, it's okay to pause and gather your thoughts during a chat.

The Buddy System

Facing social situations alone can be intimidating. Enlist a friend as your ally—it's like having a co-op partner in a video game. Having someone you trust by your side can provide comfort and make socializing less intimidating. Plus, it's always more fun to navigate the social landscape together.

Focus Outward, Not Inward

When anxiety strikes, it's easy to get caught up in your own thoughts. Shift your focus outward by paying attention to the people around you. Ask open-ended questions and actively listen to their responses. By turning your attention away from your own worries, you'll find that social situations become less about you and more about the connections you make.

Set Realistic Goals

Think of socializing as leveling up in a game. Start with achievable goals, like making eye contact or giving someone a friendly nod. As you gain experience and confidence, you can tackle bigger challenges. Gradually pushing your comfort zone can lead to surprising achievements.

Seek Professional Support

If social anxiety feels like an unbeatable boss level in a video game, consider seeking help from a trusted adult or a mental health professional. They can provide strategies and support tailored to your unique situation, helping you conquer social anxiety like a true champion.

OVERCOMING AVOIDANCE BEHAVIOR

Now we're going to talk about something that might sound a bit boring but is super important in conquering social anxiety: overcoming avoidance behavior. We all do it—avoiding chores, homework, or that awkward conversation with our parents. But guess what? It's time to break free and conquer avoidance like the champion you are!

Understanding Avoidance

First things first, what exactly is avoidance? Examples include dodging a challenging task, ignoring a problem, or procrastinating until the last minute. It might give you temporary relief, but in the long run, it only adds stress and keeps you from reaching your full potential.

The Sneaky Trap of Avoidance

Avoidance is sneaky — it can creep into your life without you even realizing it. It shows up when you're scared, anxious, or feeling unmotivated. The problem is, the more you avoid things, the stronger your avoidance muscle gets, making it even harder to face challenges later on.

Facing Fear Head-On

Guess what? Fear is totally normal! Whether it's fear of failure, rejection, or the unknown, it's part of being human. The trick is to face those fears head-on. Take small steps, like breaking down a big task into smaller, more manageable parts. This way, you can tackle each piece without feeling overwhelmed.

Embracing Imperfection

News flash: Nobody's perfect! It's okay to make mistakes and learn from them. Don't let the fear of messing up stop you from trying new things. Embrace imperfection, because that's where growth and awesomeness happen.

The Power of Positive Self-Talk

Your mind is a powerful tool, and the way you talk to yourself matters. When it comes to overcoming avoidance, try saying, "I'll give it my best shot," instead of "I can't do this." Positive self-talk can boost your confidence and help you push through challenges. Remember, you're stronger and more capable than you think!

Activity: Practice initiating a conversation with someone you don't know.

CHAPTER SEVEN:
TEST ANXIETY

WHAT IS
TEST ANXIETY?

This type of anxiety is probably not a stranger to you. It's that unsettling mix of stress and nerves that shows up when you're faced with a big exam. Think of it as the nerves you might feel before stepping onto a stage, but instead, you're armed with a pencil and paper.

The Universality of Test Anxiety

Test anxiety doesn't discriminate. It doesn't care if you're the class clown or the quiet bookworm. It can sneak up on anyone, regardless of your academic track record. It's that sneaky companion that can turn a perfectly normal day into a stress fest.

The Mental Obstacle Course

Now, let's break it down a bit. You've got a big test coming up, and suddenly your mind starts playing tricks on you. You might worry about your mind going blank, fear disappointing your parents or teachers, or stress about what your friends will think if you don't do well. It's like a mental obstacle course, and every negative thought is a hurdle you need to jump.

Physical Manifestations of Anxiety

Physically, your body might join the anxiety party too. Your heart might race, your hands get clammy, and your stomach feels like it's doing flips. It's like your body is preparing for battle, even though you're just sitting at a desk with a paper in front of you.

Normalizing Test Anxiety

Here's the thing—test anxiety is totally normal. Almost everyone feels it at some point. It's just your brain's way of saying, "Hey, this is important, pay attention!" The challenge arises when it goes into overdrive and starts making it hard for you to show what you really know.

You're Not Alone

The good news is that you're not alone. Plenty of your peers are dealing with the same beast. Feeling a little anxious is okay—it's a sign that you care about doing well.

COMMON TRIGGERS OF TEST ANXIETY

Navigating the world of test anxiety is a shared experience among teenagers. Understanding the common triggers is the first step in overcoming this challenge. From the fear of failure to the pressure of time, each trigger plays a role in shaping the way we approach exams. Let's delve into these factors together.

Fear of Failure: Navigating Expectations

One of the key triggers of test anxiety is the fear of failure. It's that pressure to meet expectations—from parents, teachers, and even ourselves. The invisible scoreboard can feel daunting, but here's the truth: It's okay not to be perfect. Mistakes are part of the learning journey, so take a deep breath and give yourself some credit.

The Comparison Game: Your Pace, Your Progress

Ever find yourself glancing around the classroom, wondering if you're the only one struggling? The comparison game is real, but here's a friendly reminder: Everyone has their own pace and strengths. Focus on your progress, not on how others are doing. You're on your unique journey, and that's something to celebrate.

Information Overload

Tests often come with an overwhelming amount of information. It can sometimes feel like trying to memorize the entire internet. Here's a secret: Focus on understanding the concepts rather than memorizing everything word for word. Break it down into smaller, manageable chunks, and suddenly, it won't seem as overwhelming.

Physical Symptoms

Sweaty palms, a racing heart, and a queasy stomach—sound familiar? These physical symptoms often accompany stress and anxiety. The key is to find ways to manage them. Deep breaths, a quick walk, or a simple stretch can do wonders to calm your nerves. Taking care of your body is just as important as taking care of your mind.

Facing the Unknown: Preparation is Power

The unknown can be anxiety-inducing—unexpected test content or format can send your mind into overdrive. The solution? Prepare as best as you can. Review your notes, ask questions, and seek help when needed. The more prepared you are, the less room there is for the unknown to stress you out.

Peer Pressure Paranoia: Feeling Judged

The watchful eyes of classmates can escalate anxiety. Fear of judgment and comparison have a way of making you question your abilities. Remember, everyone has their unique strengths, and you're on your personal academic journey. Don't let the pressure of perceived judgment cloud your focus.

Test-Taking Environment Jitters

An unfamiliar or distracting test environment can spike anxiety levels. Uncomfortable chairs, noisy surroundings, or even an overly cold room can throw you off your game. Creating a comfortable, focused space during preparation can help mitigate these environmental triggers.

COPING WITH
TEST ANXIETY

Now that we've discussed some of the more common triggers of test anxiety (besides the actual test, of course), it's time to learn some strategies for dealing with the stress.

Mindful Breathing: Inhale Confidence, Exhale Stress

When anxiety starts knocking, take a moment for some mindful breathing. Inhale slowly, count to three and exhale even slower. This simple trick can work wonders. It calms your nerves, slows your heart rate, and helps you refocus. Practice it during study breaks to build your stress-busting skills.

Break It Down: Smaller Goals, Bigger Confidence

Tests can feel like Mount Everest, but guess what? No one climbs Everest in one giant leap. Break your study material into smaller, manageable chunks. Tackle one section at a time, and watch your confidence grow as you conquer each piece. Before you know it, you'll be standing on top of that metaphorical mountain of knowledge.

Create a Study Plan: Organize and Conquer

Planning is the best weapon to combat test anxiety. Create a study plan that lays out what you'll study and when. Be realistic about your time and goals. Having a roadmap helps you stay on track, reducing last-minute cramming and the stress that comes with it.

Active Study Techniques: Engage Your Brain

Sitting for hours staring at a textbook? Not the most effective strategy, right? Try active study techniques to engage your brain. Create flashcards, teach the material to a friend, or quiz yourself. The more interactive your study sessions, the better you'll retain information. Plus, it keeps boredom at bay!

Time Management: Mastering the Clock

Ever feel rushed during a test? Mastering time management can be a game-changer. Practice timed quizzes during your study sessions to get a feel for pacing. Know how much time you have for each section and stick to it. Breaking the test into time chunks makes it more manageable and less overwhelming.

Healthy Habits: Fuel Your Brain and Body

Your brain can do amazing things that can help you with taking tests—as long as you give it the right fuel. Eat nutritious meals, stay hydrated, and get enough sleep. A well-nourished body equals a well-performing brain. Avoid the last-minute caffeine overdose; it can lead to jitters. Treat your body and mind with care, and they'll work together to help you ace that test.

Reach Out for Support: You're Not Alone

Feeling overwhelmed? It's okay to ask for help. Talk to your teachers, friends, or family. Sometimes, just sharing your worries can lighten the load. You're not alone in this journey, and there's strength in seeking support. Remember, it's okay not to have all the answers, but it's even better to ask for help finding them.

PREPARATION AND PRACTICE

Let's take a closer look at one of the best strategies for keeping text anxiety to a minimum. Adequate preparation and practice are absolute game-changers when facing challenging exams. So, why are they so important? Let's break it down.

Confidence Booster: Know Your Stuff

Picture this: You're walking into the exam room, head held high, feeling like you own the place. How does that happen? Simple—preparation! When you've put in the time to understand and master the material, you're essentially arming yourself with confidence, a weapon that no anxiety can stand up to. Knowing your stuff inside and out is your ticket to feeling capable and ready for anything that the test throws your way.

Familiarity Breeds Comfort: Reduce the Unknown

Ever been nervous about something you've never done before? It's totally normal. But here's the cool part—preparation is like turning the unknown into your best friend. When you practice regularly, the test becomes familiar territory. You've seen those types of questions, tackled those problems, and navigated those scenarios. By the time the actual test rolls around, it'll be like meeting an old friend. Familiarity breeds comfort, and comfort is your ally against anxiety.

Time Management: Taming the Clock

Imagine the clock is ticking, and you're in the middle of the test. Panic mode, right? But not for you, the time management master! Preparation and practice give you the power to master the clock. When you've done timed quizzes, practiced pacing yourself, and know how to allocate your time wisely, that ticking clock becomes your sidekick, not your enemy.

Stress-Proof Armor: Handling Curveballs

Life is full of surprises, and so are tests. But guess what? When you've prepared thoroughly, you've equipped yourself with stress-proof armor. Tough questions? Tricky scenarios? Bring it on! Your preparation has trained your brain to adapt and handle curveballs with ease, like a shield against unexpected challenges. No anxiety can penetrate that armor!

Celebrate Progress, Not Perfection

Let's be real—nobody's perfect, and that includes acing every single question on a test. Luckily, preparation and practice teach you that it's okay not to be perfect. What matters most is your progress. Celebrate the moments when you understand something new, conquer a challenging problem, or improve your study habits. The journey is where the real growth happens, and that's something worth celebrating.

Activity: Create a study schedule for an upcoming exam.

CHAPTER EIGHT: COPING WITH PANIC ATTACKS

WHAT IS A
PANIC ATTACK?

Sometimes, when anxiety gets too overwhelming, it can cause a panic attack. These can be super scary, and once you have one, the worry about having another one can increase your anxiety even further. Fortunately, there are ways to recognize the beginnings of a panic attack so you can keep it from happening, or at least mitigate its severity. Let's look a little deeper into panic attacks, then we'll teach you how to recognize when they might occur and strategies for managing them.

A panic attack is a sudden rush of intense fear and anxiety that can catch you completely off guard. Imagine you're in the middle of a regular day, and bam! Your heart starts racing, you can't catch your breath, and you feel an overwhelming sense of dread. It's like your brain hits the panic button, and you're overwhelmed with uncertainty. You might know what caused it, or you might have no idea. Panic attacks can be related to specific anxieties (like before a test or a fear of heights), or they can seem to come out of nowhere.

Why Teens?

Not everyone experiences panic attacks, but for those who do, the attacks often start during their teenage years. We're going through some major changes—hormones are all over the place, social pressures are real, and the quest to figure out who we are is in full swing—and panic attacks can complicate matters even further. It's not known exactly what factors cause panic attacks to surface, but genetics and major stress are two things that are thought to play a role.

Recognizing a Panic Attack

How do you know if it's a panic attack and not just a bad day? Good question! During a panic attack, your body goes into fight-or-flight mode, even if there's no obvious danger. The key is that these symptoms usually peak within a few minutes and then start to fade. Here are some things you might experience during a panic attack:

Racing Heartbeat: An elevated heart rate often accompanies a panic attack. Your heart might feel like it's beating twice as fast inside your chest (and it really might be!)

Shortness of Breath: Ever felt like you can't catch your breath, even if you're not exercising hard? That's a common symptom. Your breathing might become rapid and shallow during a panic attack, making you feel like you're not getting enough air.

Dizziness or Lightheadedness: Feeling a bit wobbly or like the room is spinning is another signal. Dizziness or lightheadedness can be part of a panic attack.

Muscle Tension: During a panic attack, your muscles might tense up, making you feel stiff and uncomfortable. It's like your body is preparing for danger, even if there's no apparent threat.

Feeling of Losing Control: Sometimes, you might feel like you're losing control or going crazy. It's important to remember that these feelings are temporary and part of the panic attack.

Recognizing these symptoms is the first step in managing a panic attack. If you ever notice these signs, take a deep breath, remind yourself it will pass, and consider trying some calming techniques, which we will talk more about a bit later. It's recommended to tell a trusted adult or doctor about any panic attacks you have as they are usually a sign that something deeper is going on health-wise.

COMMON TRIGGERS OF PANIC ATTACKS

As a teenager, your life may seem to be in constant flux. Just when you get a handle on one challenge, another one comes your way. One of those challenges might be panic attacks, and while you're far from the only person to experience them, it's beneficial to learn what triggers them so you can manage them better. There are many, many possible triggers for panic attacks, and the triggers vary from person to person, but we'll cover a few of them here. If you are experiencing panic attacks, talk with your parents or doctor about the triggers you notice and how best to manage them.

Academic Pressure

The pressure to excel in exams, meet deadlines, and please everyone can sometimes feel like too much. Fear of failure or an overwhelming workload can trigger a tidal wave of stress. If this pressure builds to the point that it becomes unmanageable, that might lead to experiences of panic.

Social Anxiety

The teenage years are notorious for social drama. The fear of judgment or being the odd one out is much worse for some than others and might lead to panic attacks for some people.

Family Issues

Family dynamics are often challenging, and conflicts at home can become a breeding ground for anxiety. Whether it's arguments, divorce, or strained relationships, these situations can make you feel like the ground is slipping beneath your feet. For some, this anxiety might build to the point of panic attacks.

Hormonal Changes

Ah, hormones—the enemy wizards behind mood swings and emotional instability. Puberty brings about significant hormonal changes, and sometimes, these fluctuations can trigger panic attacks.

Overwhelming Technology

In the age of social media and constant connectivity, the virtual world can become a source of stress. Cyberbullying, unfavorable comparisons, and the fear of missing out (FOMO) might contribute to anxiety and panic attacks.

Uncertain Future

Thinking about the future—career choices, college, life after high school—can be daunting. The uncertainty of what lies ahead can trigger significant anxiety and even panic.

Traumatic Events

We know life will throw curveballs occasionally, and in this book, we've talked about some ways to learn from mistakes and overcome challenges. However, sometimes the obstacles you face might be more serious than just everyday difficulties, and you shouldn't try to handle these alone. Experiencing or witnessing traumatic events, such as accidents, violence, or natural disasters, can shake the very foundation of your sense of safety. These events can trigger panic attacks, often leaving you feeling extremely vulnerable and scared. If you've been through something like this, it's crucial to seek professional help, such as therapy or counseling, to process and cope with the trauma.

Lack of Sleep

Late-night study sessions, binge-watching TV shows, or scrolling through social media into the wee hours—we've all been there. However, a lack of adequate rest can wreak havoc on your mental well-being and become a significant trigger for panic attacks. Your brain needs enough rest and a consistent sleep schedule to function correctly.

COPING WITH PANIC ATTACKS

As with anxiety, occasional panic attacks might be manageable if you know some techniques to use when you feel one coming on. These coping strategies, which you will notice are very similar to those we recommended for managing anxiety, will help you weather the storm when panic comes knocking. As always, though, it's important to seek the help of a professional if your symptoms are making it impossible to deal with.

Deep Breathing and Mindfulness

When panic strikes and your body goes into overdrive, deep breathing exercises can be a game-changer. Try the 4-7-8 technique: Inhale for a count of 4, hold for 7 and exhale for 8. This helps regulate your breathing and fosters a sense of calm. Pair this technique with mindfulness—focus on the present moment, acknowledge your feelings without judgment, and let them pass.

Create a Safe Space

Identify a safe space—physically or mentally—where you can retreat when panic sets in. It could be a cozy corner, your favorite song, or a mental image that brings comfort. Having a designated safe space provides a sense of security and control, helping you regain your composure.

Reach Out for Support

We've said this a lot and we're going to say it again: You're not alone. Reach out to friends, family, or a trusted adult when you feel a panic attack looming. Share your feelings—talking about it can alleviate the intensity. Let them know how they can support you during those moments.

Practice Progressive Muscle Relaxation

Tension often accompanies panic attacks. Progressive Muscle Relaxation (PMR) involves tensing and then gradually releasing each muscle group in your body. Start with your toes and work your way up to your head. This not only eases physical tension but also distracts your mind from panic-inducing thoughts.

Establish a Grounding Technique

Grounding techniques bring you back to reality when panic takes you to another dimension. Focus on your senses—touch, sight, hearing, smell, and taste. For example, touch a textured object, name five things you see around you, or take note of three distinct sounds. This anchors you in the present moment and interrupts the panic cycle.

Create a Panic Attack Toolkit

Prepare a toolkit of things that comfort and soothe you. This could include a favorite book, a stress ball, calming essential oils, or a playlist of uplifting tunes. Having these tools at your disposal gives you a tangible way to cope with panic attacks wherever you are.

Engage in Physical Activity

Exercise is a natural stressbuster. Whether it's a brisk walk, a dance session in your room, or a quick workout, physical activity releases endorphins, the feel-good hormones. Regular exercise also contributes to overall mental well-being, making you more resilient to stressors.

Seek Professional Help

If panic attacks become a persistent challenge, reach out for professional help. Therapists, counselors, and other mental health professionals are trained to provide support and guidance. They can help you explore the root causes of your anxiety and develop coping strategies tailored to your unique needs.

Tackling panic attacks is a marathon, not a sprint. Experiment with these strategies to discover what works best for you. You've got the strength within you to face these challenges head-on—take a deep breath and embrace the journey of self-discovery and resilience!

Activity: Practice a grounding technique, such as counting backward from 100.

CHAPTER NINE: SEEKING HELP

WHEN TO SEEK PROFESSIONAL HELP

It's normal to feel overwhelmed from time to time. However, there are times when these feelings can become too much to handle on your own. Here are some tips to help you recognize when it might be time to seek professional help for anxiety.

Unpredictable Intensity and Duration

Everyone experiences anxiety, but when your worries become more intense or last longer than usual, it's a sign that something might be amiss. If you find yourself feeling constantly on edge, unable to shake off anxious thoughts, or experiencing frequent panic attacks, it could be an indication that professional support is needed.

Interference with Daily Life

Anxiety can be disruptive, affecting your school, relationships, and daily activities. If you notice that your anxiety is making it challenging to concentrate in class, complete assignments, or maintain healthy relationships, it's crucial to seek help. A mental health professional can provide coping strategies and tools to manage these challenges effectively.

Physical Symptoms

Anxiety doesn't just affect your mind; it can manifest physically, too. Symptoms like headaches, stomachaches, muscle tension, and fatigue are common signs of anxiety. If you're experiencing these physical symptoms frequently, even in the absence of an obvious cause, it's wise to consult with a mental health professional who can help explore the root of these issues.

Social Withdrawal

If you find yourself withdrawing from friends and family, avoiding social situations, or feeling isolated, it might be a red flag. Anxiety has a way of convincing us that we're better off alone, but seeking professional help can provide the support needed to reconnect with those around you.

Changes in Sleep Patterns

Anxiety can disrupt your sleep, leading to difficulty falling asleep, staying asleep, or experiencing restful nights. If you notice significant changes in your sleep patterns, such as insomnia or excessive sleeping, it's worth discussing with a mental health professional who can address the underlying causes and help you establish healthier sleep habits.

Persistent Negative Thoughts

Constant negative thoughts or a feeling of hopelessness are signs that you may need extra support maintaining mental well-being. If you catch yourself consistently dwelling on pessimistic thoughts and struggling to see the positive side of things, a mental health professional can guide you in changing these patterns.

Difficulty Managing Stress

As a teenager, it's normal to encounter stress. However, if you find it increasingly difficult to manage stressors, big or small, seeking professional help can provide you with effective coping mechanisms and strategies.

Remember, asking for help is a sign of strength, not weakness. A mental health professional can offer valuable insights, coping tools, and a supportive space to navigate the challenges you're facing. You don't have to face anxiety alone; there are people ready to assist you on your journey to mental well-being.

FINDING A THERAPIST OR COUNSELOR

If you've decided to see a professional, the next step is identifying who that professional should be. Fortunately, there are plenty of people around you who can either give you the help you need or guide you through the process of finding the right person for that help.

You never have to be alone on this journey. Many teenagers go through similar experiences, and while there are professionals trained to help you navigate through it, the key is finding the one you click with. These tips can lead you to an amazing counselor or therapist who will join you on your quest to overcome anxiety.

Talk to Someone You Trust

Start by confiding in someone you trust, like a close friend, family member, or teacher. They can offer support and might even have suggestions for counselors or therapists.

School Resources

If you're still in school, consider checking with your school counselor or nurse. They can often point you in the right direction for professional help. Schools are increasingly recognizing the importance of mental health, so don't hesitate to reach out.

Online Resources

The internet can be a valuable tool in your search. Websites like Psychology Today, TherapyRoute, or BetterHelp allow you to search for therapists based on your location, preferences, and the issues you're dealing with. You can read profiles, learn about their expertise, and even schedule appointments online.

Ask for Recommendations

Reach out to friends, family, or even your primary care doctor for recommendations. Personal referrals can give you insight into what working with a particular therapist is like.

Insurance Coverage

If you have health insurance, check their provider directory to find therapists covered by your plan. This can help make therapy more affordable for you and your family.

Community Centers and Nonprofits

Local community centers, nonprofits, or mental health organizations may offer counseling services or be able to guide you to affordable options. They often have resources tailored specifically to teenagers.

Hotlines and Helplines

Don't underestimate the power of a phone call. Hotlines and helplines are available 24/7, and the counselors there can provide immediate support and guide you in finding a therapist in your area. It's a good idea to put these numbers in your phone well before you need them.

Consider Different Types of Therapy

There are various therapeutic approaches to dealing with anxiety, so it might be helpful to research and think about what resonates with you. Common types include cognitive-behavioral therapy (CBT), dialectical behavior therapy (DBT), and mindfulness-based therapy.

Check Reviews and Testimonials

Before making a decision, look for reviews or testimonials about the therapists you're considering. These can give you an idea of what to expect and whether the therapist's approach aligns with your needs.

Trust Your Instincts

Finally, trust your instincts. If you meet with a therapist and don't feel a connection, it's okay to try someone else. Finding the right fit is crucial for the effectiveness of therapy.

WHAT TO EXPECT IN THERAPY

You might still be hesitant to ask for help from a professional because you're worried about what goes on in a therapy session. This is a common concern, especially among teenagers, but adults worry about it, too. Let's walk through what you can expect during therapy with a professional so we can demystify the process for you.

Getting to Know You: The Initial Sessions

In the beginning, your therapist will aim to build a connection with you. They're not here to judge but to understand you better. Expect questions about your life, interests, and, of course, what brings you to therapy. It might feel a bit awkward at first, but remember, this is a safe space, and your therapist is here to support you. The more you share with them, the better they will be able to help you.

Unraveling the Anxiety Puzzle: Identifying Triggers

As you progress, you and your therapist will work together to identify the specific things that trigger your anxiety. It could be school, relationships, uncertainties of the future, or something else altogether. The goal is to shine a light on these triggers so you can better navigate and cope with them. This part can be challenging, but it's a crucial step in understanding your anxiety.

Tools for the Toolbox: Learning Coping Strategies

Therapy is not just about talking; it's about equipping yourself with tools to handle anxiety when it strikes. Your therapist might introduce you to various coping strategies, from mindfulness exercises to breathing techniques. These tools will become your allies in managing stress and anxiety in real-life situations.

Setting Realistic Goals: A Roadmap to Progress

Together with your therapist, you'll set achievable goals. These could be small steps to gradually face situations that make you anxious. Setting goals provides a roadmap for progress, and every small achievement is a victory. It's like leveling up in a video game—one step at a time—and you'll notice the positive changes.

Express Yourself: Finding Your Voice

Therapy is a space where you can express yourself freely without judgment. Whether it's talking, drawing, or writing, your therapist will encourage you to find a mode of expression that works for you. This is your time to explore and understand your emotions, helping you gain insights into the root of your anxiety.

Navigating Relationships: Communication Skills

Anxiety often affects how we relate to others. Therapy can help you build and improve your communication skills. You'll learn to express your needs, set boundaries, and navigate social situations with confidence. Effective communication can lead to stronger, more supportive relationships.

Building Resilience: Embracing Change

As you progress in therapy, you'll discover your inner strength and resilience. It's not about eliminating anxiety entirely but learning to coexist with it. Your therapist will guide you in embracing change and developing a mindset that empowers you to face life's challenges.

Keep in mind that therapy is a personal journey, and everyone's experience is unique. Be patient with yourself and celebrate the victories along the way. You're not alone in this — your therapist is your ally, helping you build the tools you need to face the world with resilience and courage.

Medication

Your therapist will give you a bunch of tools to use in managing your anxiety. However, they may also recommend treating your anxiety with prescription medication, which can really make a difference in how you feel on a daily basis. Medication isn't appropriate for everyone, so it's important to listen to the professionals' advice in this area.

When looking at medications, make sure to discuss potential side effects with your doctor. It's also a good idea to conduct your own research. You can read about other people's personal experiences online in places like forums or social media groups. Combining this with medical research will give you a good idea of the realistic pros and cons of each medication.

If you start a new medication, ask your family and closest friends for feedback on behavior changes. They might notice improvements or side effects that you didn't. For example, if your legal guardian notices you are sleeping a lot more than normal or your friend notices you are a lot less stressed than normal, you'll want to mention these observations to your doctor. This will help you gauge whether the meds are working well or not.

Activity: Discuss with a trusted adult how to find a therapist or counselor.

CHAPTER TEN: BUILDING A SUPPORT SYSTEM

SUPPORT SYSTEMS ARE IMPORTANT

A robust support system is critical for managing anxiety, especially as you go through your teenage years, but also throughout your life. It's normal to withdraw a little bit from your parents and other authority figures during your teen years, but it's important to know that your support system is still there when you need it. Of course, there are other people in your support system besides your parents. The key is to know who you can go to when you need help.

The Impact of Open Communication

Navigating anxiety can feel like a lonely journey, but it doesn't have to be. Having a support system means breaking the silence and sharing your thoughts and feelings. Open communication with friends, family, or a trusted adult creates a space where you feel heard and understood. You're not burdening others—you're inviting them into your world, and together, you can face the challenges head-on.

Validation and Understanding

Think about how you feel when you're talking to someone who just "gets it." A support system provides validation and understanding, reminding you that your feelings are real and okay. Whether it's a friend who has been through similar

108

experiences or a family member offering a listening ear, knowing you're not alone in your struggles can be a game-changer.

Emotional Support During Tough Times

Having a support system means having someone to lean on during tough times. It could be a friend sending an encouraging text, a family member offering a comforting hug, or a mentor providing guidance. Knowing you have emotional support helps you build resilience and navigate challenges more effectively.

Crisis Intervention and Professional Guidance

In moments of crisis, a support system becomes a lifeline. Friends and family can help provide immediate comfort, but sometimes professional guidance is needed. A support system can connect you with mental health professionals — therapists, counselors, or psychologists — who specialize in managing anxiety and panic attacks. Their expertise adds an extra layer of support tailored to your unique needs.

Practical Assistance: Turning Words into Actions

Support isn't just about words; it's about actions, too. Practical assistance from your support system can come in many forms. It might be a study buddy helping with school stress, a family member assisting with time management, or a friend joining you in exercise or relaxation activities. These tangible actions show that your support system is there, not just in spirit, but also in practical ways to make your journey smoother.

Fostering a Sense of Belonging

Being part of a support system fosters a sense of belonging within your community. Whether it's a tight-knit group of friends or a supportive family, having people who genuinely care creates a safety net. This sense of belonging contributes to your overall well-being, reducing the feelings of isolation that often accompany anxiety.

Encouraging Healthy Coping Mechanisms

An effective support system encourages healthy coping mechanisms. Friends might suggest engaging in hobbies together, family members may promote a balanced lifestyle, and mentors can guide you toward constructive ways of dealing with stress. Having a support system that champions healthy coping mechanisms is instrumental in managing anxiety in the long run.

You're Not Alone on this Journey

In the unpredictable teenage years, a support system is your anchor. It provides emotional support, practical assistance, and a sense of belonging. When anxiety and panic attacks threaten to overshadow your brilliance, remember that you're never alone on this journey.

IDENTIFYING SUPPORTIVE PEOPLE

Identifying supportive people in your life can make a world of difference, especially when it comes to managing anxiety. Ideally, you want multiple people you can go to during hard times. Whether you are living at home, or later in life when you have a significant other, it is important not to rely on just one person for support.

If you only have one source of support, it can be overwhelming for that person, especially if they feel responsible for your mental health. The other issue with having only one person is that they might not be available when you need them. Having multiple people you can call or turn to will increase the chances of you always being able to get ahold of someone to talk to when things get tough. It also gives you options and different types of support. Your friend might be really good at listening to you vent and hyping you up when you're struggling while an online support group can share tried and true methods for calming down from an episode.

A support group should consist of a mix of professional help (even if it's just hotline numbers in your phone), good friends you can call, in-person and online communities, spiritual or religious leaders, and family members you can trust. Here are some tips on how to spot those fantastic individuals who've got your back.

Listeners

First off, look for the listeners. Supportive people are the ones who genuinely want to hear what you have to say. They won't judge or dismiss your feelings. Pay attention to those friends, family members, or mentors who take the time to listen and ask meaningful questions. They might not have all the answers, but their willingness to lend an ear is a great sign that they care about what you're going through.

Empathy

Empathy is key. Seek out people who can put themselves in your shoes. Empathetic individuals understand that everyone faces challenges and won't dismiss your emotions as irrational. These folks will offer a shoulder to lean on and show understanding without making you feel like your feelings aren't valid. Spotting these empathetic souls can make a world of difference when you're navigating the challenges of life.

Trust

Trustworthy pals are more valuable than gold. It's essential to find people you can trust with your thoughts and feelings. Trustworthy friends won't gossip about your struggles, and they won't break your confidence. Trust is built over time, so think about how your friends handle sensitive information and whether they've proven themselves reliable in the past. Having allies you trust can significantly lighten the load when anxiety creeps in.

Cheerleaders

Look for the cheerleaders in your life. Supportive people are your biggest fans, celebrating your victories and encouraging you during tough times. Whether you've aced a test or simply made it through a challenging day, these cheerleaders uplift your spirits. Surround yourself with those who genuinely want to see you succeed and who provide encouragement when you need it the most.

Positivity

Pay attention to the positive vibes. Supportive people bring positivity into your life. They focus on your strengths and remind you of the good things, even when it's hard for you to see them yourself. Positivity is contagious, and being around people who uplift you can have a profound impact on your mental well-being.

Understanding Adults

Don't forget about understanding adults. Sometimes, talking to an adult can make a world of difference. Look for teachers, school counselors, or family members who are approachable and understanding. These adults can provide valuable guidance and support, drawing from their own experiences to help you navigate the challenges of adolescence.

Remember, it's okay to lean on others when you need help. Identifying supportive people in your life is a powerful step toward managing anxiety and building resilience. Surround yourself with those who genuinely care, listen, and uplift you. Together, you can navigate the twists and turns of life, making the journey a bit more manageable and a lot more enjoyable.

COMMUNICATING WITH SUPPORTIVE PEOPLE

Your support system can play a crucial role in helping you navigate through tough times. Effective communication is the key to ensuring they understand your needs and provide the support you require. These strategies will help keep the lines of communication clear.

Understand Your Anxiety

Before reaching out to your support system, take some time to understand your anxiety triggers and symptoms. Reflect on what situations make you anxious and how that anxiety manifests in your thoughts and feelings. This self-awareness will not only help you articulate your needs better but also enable your support system to comprehend the nature of your anxiety.

Choose the Right Time and Setting

Timing is crucial when discussing sensitive topics like anxiety. Pick a time when both you and your support people can sit down without distractions. This creates a conducive environment for open and honest communication. Avoid approaching the topic in the midst of a heated argument or during a busy family event.

Use "I" Statements

When expressing your needs, use "I" statements to avoid sounding accusatory. For example, say "I feel overwhelmed when..." instead of "You stress me out when..." This shifts the focus to your personal experience, making it easier for others to empathize and offer the support you need.

Be Specific About Your Needs

Clearly articulate what you need from your support people. Whether it's someone to talk to, a quiet space, or assistance with managing your schedule, providing specific information helps others understand how they can be of help.

Educate Your Support System

Not everyone may fully grasp what anxiety entails. Take the opportunity to educate your support system about anxiety, its symptoms, and how it affects you personally. This knowledge can bridge gaps in understanding and lead to more effective support.

Establish Boundaries

Communicate your boundaries clearly. Let your support people know what they can do to help and what actions might make your anxiety worse. This not only helps them succeed in their role but also empowers you to maintain a sense of control over your mental health.

Foster Active Listening

Encourage your support people to actively listen. This means not only hearing your words but understanding the emotions behind them. Likewise, be receptive to their feedback and suggestions. A two-way conversation fosters a supportive environment.

Develop a Crisis Plan

In moments of heightened anxiety, having a crisis plan in place can be invaluable. Work with your support system to outline specific steps or actions that can be taken when you're in distress. This proactive approach ensures everyone is on the same page and can act swiftly when needed.

Express Gratitude

When your support system provides the help you need, express gratitude. A simple "thank you" goes a long way in reinforcing the importance of their role in your life. This positive reinforcement strengthens your support system and encourages ongoing communication.

Effective communication is a skill that improves with practice. By implementing these strategies, you can foster a supportive network that plays an essential role in helping you manage your anxiety.

PEER SUPPORT GROUPS

Peer support groups are a great way to manage anxiety, and they can be especially beneficial for teens. Here are some reasons why peer support groups are helpful for teens:

Understanding and Empathy

One of the best things about peer support groups is that everyone there knows what it's like to wrestle with anxiety. It's like stepping into a room full of friends who speak the same language, and that language is empathy. People share their experiences, and suddenly, you're nodding along, thinking, "Wow, they get it!" Knowing that others are going through similar struggles makes the burden a little lighter.

Safe Space to Open Up

Imagine having a space where you can be real about what's going on in your head without fear of judgment. A good peer support group is just that—a judgment-free zone where you can share your thoughts and feelings. You don't have to be perfect; just be yourself. The relief of opening up to others who genuinely listen can be a breath of fresh air.

Learning Coping Strategies

In a peer support group, you'll discover a treasure trove of coping strategies. Whether it's mindfulness techniques, breathing exercises, or creative outlets, you'll get to try different tools to see what works best for you. Learning these techniques alongside others can make the process both easier and more fun.

Building a Supportive Network

Picture a group of friends who have your back, no matter what. That's what you get when you join a peer support group. You become part of a community where everyone supports each other. When the going gets tough, your new pals are there to lift you up. These groups are all about facing challenges together.

Gaining Perspective

Sometimes, anxiety can make everything seem overwhelming. In a peer support group, you'll meet teens who have faced similar challenges and come out stronger. Hearing their stories can give you a fresh perspective and show you that even in the toughest times, there's hope.

Celebrating Victories

Every small step forward is a victory worth celebrating. In a peer support group, your wins—no matter how big or small—are met with cheers and high-fives. It's a reminder that progress is a journey, and you're not alone in taking those steps. You're part of a team that celebrates your triumphs, making the path to managing anxiety a bit more joyful.

Joining a peer support group isn't a magical solution, but it can help you discover the strength that comes from being part of a supportive community. There are in-person groups as well as online communities. It's ideal to participate in a group that meets regularly and then join multiple support groups on social media. Social media support groups are nice because you can search for specific topics that have already been posted, ask questions for others to answer, and make more friends who are similar to you. With a little help from your peers, your battle with anxiety becomes more manageable and a lot less lonely.

Activity: Write down the names of three people you can turn to for support.

CHAPTER ELEVEN: COPING WITH CHANGE

CHANGE, TRANSITIONS, AND ANXIETY

Whether it's moving to a new school, dealing with family changes, or facing the unknowns of the future, it's completely normal to feel a bit anxious. Let's explore why change can stir up those uneasy feelings and explore ways to ride the waves of transition.

The Unknown Terrain

One major reason change causes anxiety is the fear of the unknown. It's like stepping into a mysterious forest without a map — you're not sure what lies ahead. New environments, people, and routines can be intimidating, leaving you with questions like, "Will I fit in?" or "Can I handle the challenges?" Remember, it's okay not to have all the answers right away.

Loss of Familiarity

Change often means leaving behind the familiar and stepping into uncharted territory. It's basically saying goodbye to the comfort zone you've grown accustomed to. Whether it's leaving your childhood home or transitioning to a new school, the unknown can trigger feelings of sadness, nostalgia, or even grief. It's crucial to acknowledge these emotions and give yourself time to adjust.

Peer Pressure and Comparison

Teens are no strangers to the pressures of fitting in and being accepted. When change occurs, the fear of not measuring up to the expectations of your peers can be overwhelming. It's essential to recognize that everyone experiences change differently, and there's no one-size-fits-all approach. You may feel pressured to do, say, or wear things that you don't feel comfortable with, but you need to stay true to yourself and your values. Embrace your uniqueness and don't let the fear of judgment hold you back from embracing the new opportunities that come your way, but always remember to set appropriate boundaries.

Shifting Friendships and Social Dynamics

Transitions can shake up your social circles, leading to changes in friendships and social dynamics. It's common to worry about losing old friends or struggling to make new ones. Remember that friendships evolve, and it's okay to mourn the changes while also opening yourself up to new connections. Building a support system during times of transition is crucial for navigating the challenges that come your way.

Academic Pressure and Expectations

Change often brings shifts in academic environments—new subjects, new teachers, and a more demanding workload. The fear of not meeting academic expectations can be a significant source of anxiety. Break down your tasks into manageable steps, seek help when needed, and remember that it's okay to ask questions. You're not expected to have all the answers immediately.

Change is a constant in life, and while it may bring challenges, it also opens doors to new opportunities and growth. Embrace the journey, stay true to yourself, and remember that you're not alone in facing the uncertainties of change.

COPING STRATEGIES FOR CHANGE

Now that you know why change and transition can cause anxiety, it's time for a toolkit full of strategies to help you not only cope with change but also thrive in it.

Connect with Your Feelings

Change often comes with a whirlwind of emotions. Take a moment to acknowledge and understand what you're feeling. Whether it's excitement, anxiety, or a mix of both, recognizing your emotions is the first step in coping with change. Journaling, talking to a friend, and even creating art can be great ways to express and process your feelings.

Establish a Routine

When everything around you seems to be in flux, having a routine can bring a sense of stability. Create a daily schedule that includes time for self-care, study, and relaxation. Knowing what to expect each day can provide a comforting anchor in times of uncertainty.

Break Tasks into Manageable Steps

Facing a big change can feel overwhelming, especially when it comes to new challenges. Break down your tasks into smaller, more manageable steps. Tackling one thing at a time not only makes the process less daunting but also allows you to celebrate small victories along the way.

Seek Guidance

If you find yourself struggling to cope with change, don't hesitate to seek guidance from a trusted adult, teacher, or counselor. They can offer valuable insights, support, and practical advice. Remember, it takes strength and courage to ask for help.

Celebrate Your Uniqueness

It's always easy to compare yourself to others, but this is especially true during times of transition. Remember that everyone's journey is different, and that's one of the things that makes you unique. Celebrate your individuality, embrace your strengths, and recognize that you have the power to shape your own path.

Change may be a constant, but so is your resilience and ability to adapt. Armed with these strategies, you'll be well-equipped to not only navigate change but also emerge stronger on the other side.

PREPARING FOR TRANSITIONS

Transitioning from one phase of life to another can trigger a range of emotions. It's natural to feel anxious about the unknown, but there are ways to prepare and make these transitions smoother. Here's a guide to help you navigate these changes with confidence.

Embrace the Unknown

Acknowledge Your Feelings: It's normal to feel a wide range of emotions when faced with change. Accepting these emotions is the first step in managing them. Embrace the unknown as an opportunity for growth and new experiences.

Positive Self-Talk: Replace negative thoughts with positive affirmations. Remind yourself of past successes and your ability to adapt. You've conquered challenges before, and you can do it again.

Learn About the New Environment

Research and Explore: If you're moving to a new place, take the time to research and explore. Familiarize yourself with the local community, resources, and any activities that interest you. Knowledge is a powerful tool in easing the uncertainty of the unknown.

Connect with Peers: Reach out to individuals who have experienced similar transitions. They can provide insight and advice based on their own experiences, making you feel more prepared.

Develop Time Management Skills

Create a Schedule: Establishing a routine can provide a sense of stability during the transition. Plan your day, allocate time for essential activities, and ensure you have a healthy balance between work and leisure.

Prioritize Self-Care: Don't forget to take care of yourself. Ensure you get enough sleep, eat well, and engage in activities that bring you joy. Whenever you anticipate changes or transitions, schedule more time for these activities. A healthy body and mind are better equipped to handle challenges.

A GROWTH MINDSET

In the previous section, we mentioned that a growth mindset can help you manage the anxiety that comes with change. Developing a growth mindset is like unlocking a secret code that empowers you to face challenges with resilience and enthusiasm. Let's talk about how you can cultivate a growth mindset and take control of your change-related anxiety.

Effort is the Key to Mastery

Success doesn't happen overnight. It's the result of consistent effort and hard work. Instead of focusing solely on the end goal, appreciate the journey and the progress you make along the way. Whether it's acing a test or mastering a musical instrument, recognize that effort is the driving force behind your achievements.

Cultivate a Love for Learning

Curiosity is your superpower! Embrace the joy of discovery and foster a love for learning. Seek out new experiences, explore different subjects, and be open to gaining knowledge from various sources. The more you immerse yourself in learning, the more resilient and adaptable you become in the face of challenges.

Emphasize the Power of "Yet"

"I can't do this . . . yet." Adding the word "yet" to your vocabulary transforms a statement of limitation into one of potential. Recognize that your abilities are not fixed, and with time, effort, and dedication, you can develop any skill and overcome any obstacle. The power of "yet" opens doors to endless possibilities.

Activity: Write down one thing you are looking forward to in the future.

CHAPTER TWELVE: MOVING FORWARD

THE IMPORTANCE
OF REFLECTION

As you've made your way through this book, you have already begun to conquer your anxiety. At this time, you should take a few minutes to reflect on the progress you've made so far because you have made progress.

Why Reflect on Your Progress?

Awareness is Power: Reflecting on your anxiety journey is like turning on the light in a dark room. It gives you a clear view of what's going on. By recognizing your emotions, triggers, and coping mechanisms, you gain the upper hand in managing anxiety.

Identify Patterns: Anxiety often follows patterns. Maybe it intensifies during exams, social events, or specific situations. Reflecting helps you spot these patterns. Once you recognize them, you can work on strategies to navigate those challenging moments more effectively.

Track Your Growth: Imagine looking back at a photo from a year ago and realizing how much you've grown. Reflecting on your anxiety journey is similar. It allows you to see the progress you've made, reminding you that you're on a path of personal growth and resilience.

HOW TO REFLECT ON YOUR PROGRESS

Keep a Journal

Start a journal where you jot down your thoughts and feelings regularly. It's like having a conversation with yourself. Note moments when you felt anxious, what triggered it, and how you coped. Over time, this journal becomes the story of your progress.

Learn and Adapt

Life is a continuous learning process. Reflect on what strategies work best for you and which ones need tweaking. Be open to trying new approaches and adapting your coping mechanisms. It's all about finding what suits you best.

Reflecting on your anxiety journey is not about perfection; it's about progress. Embrace the process, celebrate your victories, and keep moving forward.

MAINTAINING PROGRESS

You've embarked on this journey of managing anxiety and now have a toolkit full of fantastic strategies. You've also undoubtedly made progress in learning how to keep your anxiety at bay.

However, as with anything that's challenging, there will be moments when quitting seems tempting. Let's talk about how you can keep going even when the going gets tough.

Anchor Yourself in Your Why

Why did you start this journey in the first place? Remind yourself of the reasons behind your commitment to managing anxiety. Whether it's better mental health, improved relationships, or personal growth, having a clear "why" serves as your North Star, guiding you through challenging times.

Create a Visual Reminder

Visualize your journey. Consider creating a vision board or a simple visual reminder of your goals and the progress you've made. When the going gets tough, a glance at this visual representation can reignite your motivation and remind you of your resilience.

Adjust and Adapt Strategies

Flexibility is your ally. If a particular strategy doesn't seem to be working as expected, don't hesitate to adjust and adapt. You're not failing; you're learning. Experiment with different approaches until you find what works best for you. It's all part of the process.

Visualize a Positive Future

Envision the positive outcomes that await you on this journey. Picture yourself overcoming challenges, experiencing joy, and living a life that aligns with your values. This positive visualization can serve as a powerful motivator, inspiring you to push through the tough times.

The path to managing anxiety is certainly challenging, but your ability to persevere is what will see you through. Embrace the journey, stay connected to your "why," and remember that every step forward is a triumph.

THE IMPORTANCE OF SELF-COMPASSION

You've learned some incredible strategies to manage your anxiety, and now the time has come to put them into action on your own. It's a thrilling and slightly nerve-wracking chapter of your story, but fear not—you've got the tools, and we're here to remind you of the importance of self-compassion as you venture out into the world.

It's Okay to Feel Nervous

Heading out to practice your anxiety-management strategies independently might stir up some nerves, and guess what? That's okay! Acknowledge your feelings and remember that feeling nervous doesn't diminish your capabilities. It's a sign that you're stepping outside your comfort zone and embracing growth— bravery only exists in the face of fear.

Stay Present

As you face new challenges, remember the power of mindfulness. Stay present in the moment, focusing on your breath and the task at hand. Mindfulness isn't just a tool for meditation; it's a practical skill you can apply to real-life situations. By staying present, you'll navigate challenges with a calm and centered mind.

You've Got the Skills, Now Trust Yourself

As you begin practicing anxiety-management strategies independently, carry with you the tool of self-compassion. Reflect on your progress, acknowledge your feelings, apply mindfulness, celebrate successes, be gentle with yourself, build a supportive environment, and embrace the learning process. You've got the skills, and most importantly, you've got strength within you. Trust yourself, believe in your capabilities, and know that you're fully equipped for this exciting solo adventure.

Activity: Write down one goal for managing anxiety moving forward.

CONCLUSION

Congratulations! You've reached the final chapter of the *Anxiety Survival Guide for Teens*, and hopefully, this journey has equipped you with the tools and knowledge you need to conquer the dragons of anxiety that may have threatened your path.

As you reflect on the insights shared within these pages, remember that resilience is your greatest ally. Life's challenges may not vanish, but armed with newfound strategies, you have the power to face them head-on. Embrace the idea that it's okay to stumble, to feel anxious, and to ask for support. You are not alone in this adventure, and seeking help is a strength, not a weakness.

Mindfulness, breathing exercises, and the art of self-reflection are now your trusty companions. They provide solace when the storm of stress looms large. Cultivate these practices, make them your own, and watch as they become second nature, helping you find peace amidst chaos.

As you close this book and step back into the world, carry with you the knowledge that you are stronger than you think, more resilient than you feel, and destined for greatness. The journey of self-discovery doesn't end here; it's an ongoing adventure filled with twists, turns, and triumphs.

Remember, this guide is not just a book; it's a companion for life. Revisit its pages whenever the shadows of anxiety threaten to creep back in. You are the hero of your story, and with the lessons learned here, you possess the courage to face any challenge that comes your way.

www.ingramcontent.com/pod-product-compliance
Lightning Source LLC
Chambersburg PA
CBHW060236030426
42335CB00014B/1489